ABOVE: *White poinsettia*
PREVIOUS PAGE: *Dills Falls framed by Fraser firs, West Fork of the Pigeon River, Haywood County*

# A North Carolina Christmas

Written and Compiled by
**JAN KIEFER**

Foreword by
**WILLIAM FRIDAY**

Featuring Photography by
**GEORGE HUMPHRIES**
and
**DAVID CROSBY**

Published by
**WESTCLIFFE PUBLISHERS, INC.**
**ENGLEWOOD, COLORADO**

*I WOULD LIKE TO EXPRESS SPECIAL THANKS TO:*
*My mother, Charlotte, who spent many hours keystroking and*
*making phone calls, as well as helping greatly with the taste test.*

*My lifelong friend Beth, who not only helped me gather*
*information, but also advised me about many important issues*
*regarding North Carolina.*

*My brother Robert and his wife, Patricia, who organized the*
*taste test and made it happen despite the Blizzard of 1996.*

*My friends Shirley and Jan, who have shared the highs*
*and lows and continually encouraged me.*

*—J.K.*

EDITOR: Suzanne Venino
DESIGNER: Rebecca Finkel, F + P Graphic Design
PRODUCTION MANAGER: Pattie Coughlin

© 1996 Jan Kiefer. ALL RIGHTS RESERVED.

FOREWORD BY
© 1996 William Friday. ALL RIGHTS RESERVED.

PHOTOGRAPHY BY
© 1996 George Humphries. ALL RIGHTS RESERVED.
© 1996 David Crosby. ALL RIGHTS RESERVED.

INTERNATIONAL STANDARDS BOOK NUMBER
1-56579-154-1

LIBRARY OF CONGRESS CATALOG NUMBER
96-60391

PUBLISHED BY
Westcliffe Publishers, Inc.
2650 South Zuni Street
Englewood, Colorado 80110

PRINTED IN HONG KONG BY
PALACE PRESS INTERNATIONAL

*No portion of this book, either photographs*
*or text, may be reproduced in any form without*
*the written permission of the publisher.*

*All items in this book were either submitted as*
*original material or are reprinted with permission.*
*Neither Westcliffe Publishers nor Jan Kiefer is*
*responsible for any misrepresentation of origin.*

*Cabin in the snow, Starnes Cove, Buncombe County*

# TABLE OF
# CONTENTS

## Foreword

Christmas we remember as that warm, wonderful time in our lives when families gather around the hearth for good food, holiday gifts, and, most of all, renewing the real spirit of the Christmas season. It is just good to be together.

On these pages are the scenes and remembrances of this most joyful of all seasons. Those of us who live in this wonderful state will find in George Humphries's photographs many reminders of our good fortune. He reminds us also of our stewardship of this glorious environment and of our own gift to succeeding generations of a yet more protected land and sea, rivers and sky.

Christmas in North Carolina is wreaths and carolers, the excitement of children, snow and sleds, snow cream made the old fashioned way, turkey and cornbread dressing, preserves and leftovers that still taste good. It is a time of giving and caring and sharing with our neighbors.

Carolinians remember the real message of this splendid season. They sing the great carols in their neighborhood churches with gratitude for the eternal message of good will and joy among all of us all over the world. With childlike wonder we marvel at the power of the season to renew and restore the best within us.

So settle back by the fire, give yourself a treat, open up your memory and your heart, and enjoy the rich journey that is yours as you turn these pages of *A North Carolina Christmas*. You will be glad that you did.

*William Friday*

*William Friday is the former president of the University of North Carolina system. He currently hosts the T.V. show* North Carolina People. *He is also the Executive Director of the William R. Keenan, Jr. Charitable Trust Foundation.*

*The Richmond Hill Inn, Asheville*

# Preface

I came down from the mountain one December afternoon. The remnants of an early North Carolina winter snow wrapped like woolen blankets a.ound the trees and hung off the rocks along Highway 321 in great, jagged ice floes. A dreamsicle-colored sky lent rows and rows of Blue Ridge Mountains a frost-fire haze in the late day. It's the time of year when the sun doesn't hurt your eyes as it lowers itself in gaudy orange through the depressions created by the gently curving peaks.

Tranquillity washed over me as I pushed one of my favorite Christmas tapes into the player. A chorus of male voices boomed at me, "And in despair I bowed my head/There is no peace on earth I said/For hate is strong and mocks the song/Of peace on earth, Good Will to men." Rude awakening, I thought, in the middle of all nature's glory. Then the full chorus came back with the lovely affirmation, "Then pealed the bells more loud and deep/God is not dead, nor doth He sleep/For wrong shall fail and right prevail/With peace on earth, Good Will to men."

The Christmas holidays are a time of reaffirmation. It is the time when people reflect on the past and put forth hope for the future. At Christmastime, the old traditions aren't so "old-fashioned" anymore, family is the right place to be, and we are reminded again that peace and good will are qualities to be sought. These days peace on earth is an illusive thing; still the spirit of Christmas can be found everywhere—and nowhere more deeply than in the hearts and homes of the people of North Carolina.

From hidden hollows and soaring peaks in the mountains to the rolling farms and great cities of the piedmont and plains, to the meandering inlets, swamps, and picturesque communities of the coast, the people of North Carolina celebrate the season. Some celebrate quietly in their homes and churches, carrying on traditions ancestors brought over from England, Europe, or Africa. Others are out in force, taking advantage of the many opportunities to celebrate in groups. Throughout the state, there is that great, good feeling of brotherhood. Whether it's singing in a choir, attending a concert or a parade, or shooting their guns in celebration, North Carolinians don't let anything hold them back.

That's what this book is all about—a look at the entire state of North Carolina at Christmas: its citizens, its celebrations, its food, its history, its music, its humor. Not a definitive study, rather the intention of this book is to weave together a holiday tapestry, pulling the various threads together into a beautiful pattern. I hope that feeling of peace I felt coming down the mountain will pervade your spirit as you enjoy *A North Carolina Christmas.*

*Jan E. Kuifer*

*OPPOSITE: Fine's Creek Memorial Baptist Church, Haywood County*

*This book is dedicated to the first North Carolinians I ever knew and loved—
my classmates at the Ben Lippen School in Asheville, class of 1964.*

Tom, Rick, Bo, Bob, Dottie, Ralph, Murray, Beth, Grace, Madge, Harold,
Nat, Igou, Lee, Tom, Bill, Alleene, Joy, Ralph, David, Lenny, Daisy, Keith,
Ron, Cheryl, Sharon, Lois, Bill, Bob, Jane, Luann, Caroline and Jim.

—J.K.

# Christmas Came to North Carolina

The history of Christmas in North Carolina is as varied as its citizens themselves. This wonderful diversity began to emerge during the mid-1700s, when much of the colony was considered frontier. The earliest settlers were primarily of English decent, but as word of plentiful land and religious tolerance spread back to the British Isles, there was a noticeable influx of Highland Scots, Scots-Irish, and Welsh. The pious English and Scots saw Christmas as a time for prayer and reflection. The arrival of immigrants from Europe, primarily German Lutherans, brought more exuberant Christmas celebrations. With the slave trade from Africa and the West Indies, slaves often embraced the religion of their owners, adapting it to their own style of worship.

The Great Wagon Road encouraged settlers from the northern colonies to migrate south. In 1752, a party of Moravians from the thriving settlements of Bethlehem and Nazareth in Pennsylvania headed southward. Having left the women and children behind, the men were going on ahead to establish a new settlement in North Carolina. They purchased nearly 10,000 acres from Lord Granville in the piedmont of North Carolina, including much of what is now the city of Winston-Salem.

*Historic Gemeinhaus, Bethabara*

Called the Brethren, the Moravians established the settlement of Bethabara ("House of Passage" in Hebrew) and celebrated their first Christmas in a log house. They held a service in the morning and concluded with their traditional love feast, sharing food and fellowship among themselves. Music was integral to the celebration, as it was to the Moravian's every day life. Early records tell of a wooden trumpet, a small organ, French horns, and violins played during the love feast.

The following was documented in one of the early Moravian journals:

> On Christmas Day the English children from the mill came to see our Christmas decoration; they were so poorly clad that it would have moved a stone to pity. We told them why we rejoiced like children and gave to each a piece of cake. In Bethania Brother Ettwein held a Love-feast for the twenty-four children there; at the close of the service each received a pretty Christmas verse and a ginger cake, the first they had ever seen.

Within two years, the Moravians were holding regular Christmas love feasts for the children. At the end of the service, children were each given a candle to remind them that they should be a shining light for God. By the 1760s, the largest of the Moravian settlements was established and named Salem, or "peace." The love feast has been celebrated by the Moravians for more than two hundred years. It is a beautiful ceremony still observed today.

*Christmas music at Old Salem, where the trombone is thought to have originated*

In 1752 the British Crown directed all its colonies, including North Carolina, to change over to the Gregorian calendar, which observed Christmas on December 25. The residents of Rodanthe on the Outer Banks, had observed the traditional Old English Christmas, although they celebrated on January 5, not January 6, as was customary. They paraded around the settlement, beating drums, playing fifes, and scaring off "Old Buck," a terrifying creature resembling a huge bull. Old Buck ran around, stomping and snorting, pawing the ground and chasing children. Legend had it that he knew which children had been good and which ones bad, and Old Buck was particularly threatening to those who had been bad. It was said he haunted the Trent Woods, and children would shout out, "It's Old Buck! Old Buck's coming out of Trent Woods."

These days, the celebration of old Christmas has become more of a giant homecoming for Rodanthe residents, and somewhat of a tourist attraction. One thing that hasn't changed is the consumption of oysters and other fresh seafood and holiday fare as the whole community

*Re-enactment of colonial Christmas at Fort Defiance, near Lenoir*

*Christmas dinner at Fort Defiance includes St. Lucia's Crown for desert*

gathers together. Old Buck is not nearly so frightening now, and children especially enjoy the fact that they can observe both old Christmas and new Christmas.

As North Carolina moved into the 1800s, rapidly becoming populated with cities in the central and eastern regions and towns in the west, new holiday practices began to appear. On the great eastern plantations, slaves were often permitted time off from work, sometimes as long as the great yule log burned. This resulted in the practice of the slaves producing the biggest, most water-soaked log they could find, which would sometimes burn for several days.

In the Wilmington area, slaves (and after 1863, former slaves) dressed up in Halloween-like costumes with grotesque masks. They traveled in groups around the town, chanting, playing instruments, snapping whips, and trailing great long streamers wherever they went. They sang and danced for townsfolk they met in the streets, but they mostly performed at people's houses. Children and adults gave them fruit, candy, small gifts, or even coins. The "Kuners," as they were called, thrived and expanded to the towns of Edenton and Hillsborough. The exact origin of the Kuners is uncertain, but it is linked to John Cannu, a great folk hero of the 1700s from the Guinea coast. Jamaicans and Bahamians arriving at Wilmington's seaport spread his fame, and his name became associated with the "kuners." Eventually, influential townspeople frowned on the practice and it gradually died out.

In 1881 the North Carolina General Assembly declared Christmas an official holiday. Celebrations, which had been held privately for many years, were now more public and more lively, with dancing, singing, and eating. Attending church services, visiting friends and family, and a whirl of parties became the standard practice.

One of the most exuberant holiday practices is still found in Cherryville, where descendants of settlers fire antique muskets, essentially "greeting" each house with a din of noise and smoke at New Year's. This practice is accompanied by a chant, hailing the season as well as the family to be greeted. Named the "New Year's Shooters," they choose a different route each year. Beginning as the bell strikes midnight, they hail each home along the route. If three shouts of "Hallo" do not bring any response, the party moves on. But in general, doors are flung open, and the shooters are warmly welcomed. Shooting guns has also been customary in many parts of the mountains, and has occasionally been attributed to the influence of moonshine, which flowed plentifully during the holiday season. Modern day shooters have been known to substitute firecrackers for gun fire.

Many pockets of tradition persist throughout North Carolina as the twentieth century ends. Rich in diversity, these holiday customs reflect the backgrounds of those who have gone before. Each generation adds its imprint and passes it on. One thing is certain—from the mountains to the coast and everywhere in between, North Carolinians have some of the most interesting, tasty, and beautiful Christmas celebrations found anywhere in the country.

*It was a thrill on Christmas morning. My father would always shoot the hunting gun over the house three times to wake us up. Everyone in the neighborhood enjoyed it.*

**—DOLLY WHISNANT,** *Lenoir*

# I Wonder as I Wander

John Jacob Niles, the singer and collector of folk songs, said that he based his
"I Wonder As I Wander" on a line or two of haunting music that he heard sung
by a young girl in a small North Carolina town. He asked her to sing the few
notes over and over, paying her a few pennies each time, until he had jotted it
down in his notebook. So close was the finished song to its Appalachian inspira-
tion that Niles is often cited as arranger of the tune rather than its creator.

— READER'S DIGEST

Reprinted by permission from the *Reader's Digest Merry Christmas Songbook*,
Copyright © 1984, The Reader's Digest Association, Inc.

*Beacon Heights, Avery County*

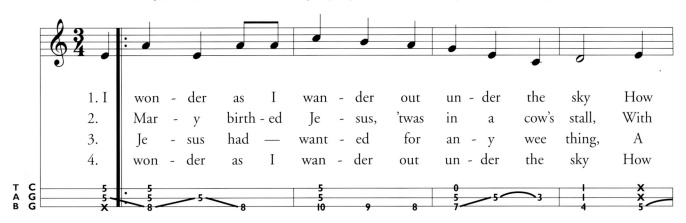

*Words and music by John Jacob Niles; arranged for fretted dulcimer by William G. Spencer*

*Suggested Strum — strum all strings on the first of each measure. Also sounds nice "picking style" using an eight note rhythm.*

*Use 6½ if you have it

"I Wonder as I Wander"
Copyright ©1934 (renewed) by G. Schirmer, Inc. (ASCAP)
International copyright secured. All rights reserved. Reprinted by permission.

# The Dulcimer Maker

On an unexpectedly warm December day, up in the hollow by Laurel Creek, just outside of Sugar Grove, you might hear the lovely haunting notes of the Appalachian fretted dulcimer. Laurel Creek is where the Glenn family creates some of the most sought-after handmade dulcimers in the world.

Leonard Glenn began making dulcimers more than forty years ago, working from a pattern passed down from his grandfather. As Leonard's son Clifford grew up, he learned the trade from his father. Together they made dulcimers and banjos to meet an ever-growing demand, first from around Appalachia and now from all over the world. These days Leonard makes only a few instruments a year, while Clifford has taken over the workshop and produces about fifty annually.

Clifford's wife, Maybelle, plays a dulcimer that was a gift from her husband, lovingly crafted from a hundred-year-old piece of cherry wood rescued from a bridge. Deep in color and rich in tone, it is delicately inlaid with gold around the heart-shaped holes.

The style known as the North Carolina dulcimer has an hourglass shape with heart-shaped holes. It is made from

*Dulcimer maker Leonard Glenn and his wife, Clara, on their porch in Laurel Creek*

native woods such as cherry, maple, beech, poplar, butternut, birch, or chestnut. Usually it has three strings, although sometimes four. And out of those shapes and holes and strings pour the very heart and soul of the mountain people.

Dulcimer music is greatly loved in the Appalachian Mountains of North Carolina, for it is like the people themselves—uncomplicated and honest. Dulcimers are played at family get-togethers, for private enjoyment, and often as solo or accompaniment in church. Particularly lovely on the dulcimer is the North Carolina Christmas song, "I Wonder as I Wander." It is hard to imagine anywhere where the words seem more appropriate than in the hollow up at Laurel Creek, outside of Sugar Grove.

*Clifford and Maybelle Glenn playing dulcimers*
*OPPOSITE: Road to Linville Falls,*
*Blue Ridge Mountains*

# O Carolina Christmas Tree

"How lovely are thy branches," we sing in the old familiar German carol. Every year more than seven million people, representing every state in the union and foreign countries as far away as Japan, agree with this sentiment. North Carolina Christmas trees are highly prized for their beauty. While some people choose the white pine and others the traditional cedar as their Christmas tree, ninety-five percent of North Carolinians select the lovely Fraser fir. So beautiful is this tree that in the past three decades it has been chosen seven times to be the official Christmas tree at the White House.

The Fraser fir is the ideal Christmas tree. It has a lovely dark green color, it is dense and thick with strong boughs and soft needles, it is easily sheared into the perfect Christmas tree shape, and, best of all, it has an enticing holiday aroma. All that, and the Fraser fir is relatively fire resistant!

Often called the "she-balsam," the tree was discovered by biologist John Fraser in mid-1800s on Mount Mitchell. The Southern Appalachian region, primarily North Carolina, is the only place in the world the Fraser fir grows naturally, for it must have exactly the right combination of altitude (above 3,500 feet), moisture, and temperature to thrive.

Just thirty years ago the Fraser fir was unknown as a Christmas tree. From its beginnings as a cash crop that could be grown in poor mountain regions, the Fraser fir has brought the state of North Carolina to rank third in U.S. Christmas tree production, bringing in revenues of more than $90 million a year.

Today North Carolina boasts more than 2,500 growers in the six northwestern counties, which have ideal conditions for growing Fraser firs. A drive through Allegheny or Ashe counties tells the story vividly. Hillside after hillside is neatly arranged with rows of the trees in various stages of growth, like thousands of soldiers standing at attention.

According to Pat Wilke, executive director of the North Carolina Christmas Tree Association, growing Fraser firs is not an easy job. After three years as seedlings and two more as transplants

*ABOVE: Harvesting Fraser firs*
*LEFT: A Fraser fir against a Blue Ridge sunset*

in the nursery, the trees are then planted in the field, where they will stay for another seven to eight years. Growers spend a great deal of time keeping their crops disease and insect free. Trees must be sheared every year to achieve that perfect Christmas-tree shape, and it has been estimated that each tree is handled more than a hundred times before it is harvested.

When the trees reach an approximate height of six feet, they are ready for harvesting, which starts the second week in November. Many people venture to the mountains to pick their own trees, and Choose 'n Cut weekends have become popular in mountain towns and surrounding communities.

The State Capitol and the Governor's Mansion in Raleigh display beautiful Fraser firs at Christmastime, as do inns and businesses all across the state. The historic Grove Park Inn in Asheville decorates nearly fifty Fraser fir trees, with the tree in the Grand Hall measuring over twenty feet tall. For its one hundredth anniversary in 1995, the Biltmore House displayed thirty-five Fraser firs, and also decorated the estate with 200 wreaths and 21,000 feet of roping—all from North Carolina.

North Carolinians lavish their homes with the natural beauty and the fresh aroma of evergreen. The Fraser fir has been cultivated here for only thirty years, yet it has become a holiday tradition for people all across the great Christmas tree state of North Carolina and beyond.

> *The Christmas tree grower stood*
> *at the pearly gate*
> *His head was bent and low*
> *He merely asked*
> *the man of fate*
> *Which way he ought to go.*
> *"What have you done,"*
> *Saint Peter asked,*
> *"To seek admittance here?"*
> *"I ran a Christmas tree farm*
> *down on earth*
> *For many and many a year."*
> *Saint Peter opened wide the gate*
> *and gently pressed the bell,*
> *"Come in," he said,*
> *"and choose your harp —*
> *You've had your share of hell."*
>
> **—ANONYMOUS**

*First Lady Hillary Clinton accepts the 1995 White House*
*Christmas tree from North Carolina growers*

*My brother raised Christmas trees*
*on our mountain land each year.*
*We always decorated the family tree*
*with momentos of special events in*
*our lives.*

**—GLORIA HOUSTON**
*author of* The Year of the
Perfect Christmas Tree

Getting and decorating the tree is a big time in our house. After Christmas, we decorate the tree a second time with pine cones covered with peanut butter and birdseed for our feathered friends. Placing it outside the window gives us an instant bird feeder in the spirit of the season, as well as an eventual animal habitat in the woods.

—**DAVID CROSBY,** *Hickory*

*We were so poor as children that our tree ornaments were made out of cut-up Coke cans. We made stars and bells and hung them on the tree along with strings of berries and popcorn and red-and-green paper chains. I still string berries and popcorn and make paper chains.*

— **M.E.B.,** *Cherokee*

# An Unforgettable Tree
## by Burnette Beam Norris, Shelby

In the Piedmont region of North Carolina, preparations for Christmas began with gathering holly. While not rare, holly trees were not plentiful, which probably accounted for the ongoing argument I had with my friend Edith about a holly tree growing on the line between our fathers' pastures. The trunk of the tree was on Beam land, but a goodly portion of the branches spread over the Davis pasture, and Edith claimed those as hers. I regret that I have more than a hazy recollection of boasting that where the tree stood was a land grant to my ancestors from the King of England, as though that had anything to do with the preponderance of evidence. It was lively conversation for eight-year-old girls, but we never came to blows, just argued. We both claimed the tree, climbed it, and wrested branches from it, snagging our clothing and skinning our limbs. It had red berries only at Christmastime, sometimes only a few, but for years it was the source of our holly decorations at Christmas.

Then I found the unforgettable tree. It was about six feet tall, perfectly shaped, growing wild in a remote corner of Beam pasture, and it was loaded with red berries the year round. I showed it to Edith and forbade her to break off one little sprig. Pride of undisputed ownership must have gone to my head. I not only bragged about the tree, but I became obsessed with the idea of having it as a Christmas tree. I revealed my secret to Edith, fully aware of her envy, and solicited her help to cut it down and bring it to the house. She agreed reluctantly, which I assumed was because she wished it were hers.

With a pocketknife and a somewhat dull butcher knife, we tackled the job of cutting it down. Holly is a tough wood, and even though the trunk was barely three inches in diameter, it resisted our efforts to take it off the hillside forever. We struggled, and once we started hacking it, we had to finish the job. I believe I would have gnawed the last remaining strands of wood with my teeth to finalize its severance.

The tree was too big for two eight-year-old girls to carry, never mind the prickly leaves scratching all our bare spots. We had to drag it over hills and through woods to the house. It was distressing to look behind us and see red berries dropping on the ground as we dragged it along.

Mother thought the tree was beautiful, and so did my sisters, who helped me put it on a stand and decorate it. Icicle tinsel and strands of popcorn were its main decorations, needing little else.

> I remember the simple joys
> of Christmas past,
> We children with handsaw
> and a choice cedar tree in mind
> Went forth across pasture and fields
> passing up one after another
> Until we found just the right one.
> Two boards tacked to the
> bottom of the tree;
> We stood it there in the
> corner of the room.
> —**Henry Lathan,** *Hudson*

*Mama always decorated the house with fresh holly with beautiful red berries, pine cones, and running moss all from the woods.*

—**Thelma Beasley,** *Westfield*

When we showed it to Daddy that evening, he had little to say. Something about his silence made me uneasy. Deep inside of me I think I knew it was wrong to cut the tree down.

Daddy waited until later in the evening when he and I were alone by the fireside. Not taking his eyes off the flickering flames, he said, "Burnette, do you know how many years it takes to grow a holly tree that size?" His voice was low and even-toned.

"Right many, I guess." I wished he would whip me.

"That tree has been growing there in the pasture since about the time you were born—eight or nine years." He paused.

It was so quiet I could hear the fire crackling. Right then I would have given anything I owned to have the tree back in the pasture.

"I guess I shouldn't have cut it down," I admitted. "I'm sorry I did it, Daddy. I thought it would be such a pretty Christmas tree for all of us. I should have asked you first, huh?"

"You most certainly should have," he said emphatically, looking directly at me. "But it's down now, its life is over, and nobody can put it back. You know there are very few holly trees like that. I want you to understand that when things are scarce, especially growing things, they need to be protected."

The conversation was ended, and we were both sad.

It was my first lesson in conservation, and, more importantly, in humility. I could see myself swaggering around in front of Edith, bragging about the tree and trying to make her jealous. I was so ashamed of what I had done. Suddenly the tree lost its magic for me. I was tired of it before Christmas arrived. I could hardly wait to take it down.

Visions of that beautiful holly tree growing on the hillside shining red in the sunlight will always be vivid to me, but what has kept it more alive was my father's forbearance and kindness toward my thoughtless deed.

*This story took place on the Beam family farm near Shelby. Four sisters and two brothers grew up on the old homestead, where Burnette has since returned to live. Now she only uses holly to decorate the mantel.*

*What's special about the holidays is our Christmas tree and opening presents with our entire family (thirteen people) on Christmas Day.*

**—CHARLES E. CORDELL**
*Asheville*

*At Christmas we would go to the woods and cut the prettiest cedar tree we could find. We would also make ornaments out of holly and ground cedar, or whatever we found in the woods.*

**—DOLLY WHISNANT,** *Lenoir*

*Wayne Ayers surveys his tree farm, with trees almost ready for harvesting*

*I grew up in Candler, where we lived in the old family homestead until it burned down when I was in the third grade. My Daddy had six sisters, and every Christmas the whole family stayed at our house for the holidays. We had no running water and only an outside johnny. Needless to say the house was crowded, but it was a lot of fun.*

*Before Christmas Daddy would take me and my brother and sister up on the mountain and we would pick out a beautiful big cedar. Daddy hunted and was an excellent shot, and he would shoot off the top of the tree because the lower branches were bare.*

**—JANE PRUDEN,** *Asheville*

*On a tree farm, the whole family selects a tree in what has become known as Choose 'n Cut*

In the fifties in Lexington there were more dirt roads than paved ones. Homes had high ceilings, tin roofs, rattling window panes, wood cook stoves, and some still had outhouses. A lot of folks believed the good Lord never meant for nature calls to be answered under the same roof where you slept and ate.

Come Christmas we just went out in the woods, chopped down a tree, broke off holly branches, shot mistletoe out of tree tops, and pulled up running cedar. I remember being out with Grandpa and I was pulling up running cedar and found a Mason jar full of water. Couldn't figure why a new jar would be in the woods so I asked Grandpa. He took the jar and mumbled something 'bout Christmas cheer. Course I didn't know about moonshiners then, and I was so excited bringing in Christmas decorations I forgot all about the jar.

**—BERNICE L. COUCH,** *Winston-Salem*

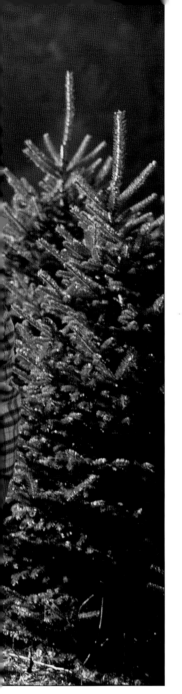

## TWICE STOLEN TREE
### A TRUE STORY
*by Russell Newell, Ocracoke*

In my town when you wanted a Christmas tree you just went out and cut one. They grew along ditches, fence lines, and on the edge of the woods. Farmers without bush hogs to dig up the trees thought you were doing them a favor.

C.L. was in his favorite chair when his wife said to him. "I don't know your plans for Christmas, but I sure don't want that plastic tree up again this year. You go out and cut one. One that smells good."

The next day C.L. went over to Bud's house. "Come on, Bud. Let's go drive around. I've got to find my wife a tree that smells good before she gets all wound up."

They looked in all the best places. "With them new bush hogs there's not a cedar tree to be found in Wilmington County," said Bud. It was almost dark when they finally saw a tree, but by all rules it was out of bounds. The tree was too close to the house and too close to the road. "It sure looks nice," said C.L. "I'll tell you what we'll do. I'll get out and cut the tree and then jump in the ditch. Bud, you go down the road and turn around. When you come back, I'll throw the tree in the back and we'll be off."

Sure enough C.L. cut the tree with two licks and jumped into the ditch with the tree. When Bud came by he had all kinds of traffic behind him and he had to give C.L. a fly-by. Then there were no cars but also no Bud. A truck was approaching, but C.L. didn't think it sounded like his, so he slithered out of the ditch and into the cornfield. Sure enough that truck came by real slow. The man seemed to see the tree and then stopped and backed up. He put the tree in the truck and drove away.

C.L. walked out into the road just when Bud drove up. "Where's the tree?" Bud asked. "Can you believe it?" said C.L. "That man just stole that Christmas tree we just stole. There ought to be a law."

The next day Bud went by to see C.L. He was in his favorite chair and the plastic tree was up. Bud looked at the scrawny cedar wreath over the fire place. "That's for smelling," said C.L.

*Christmas trees were about the only decoration we had when I was a child. We would go to the woods and find the nicest tree we could and decorate it with lights, ornaments, and tinsel. Our trees were not the perfectly symmetrical, cultivated ones of today, but they were real, not artificial. They were sparsely decorated but they were beautiful to a child's eyes. I remember one year I insisted that the tree be put up so early that it dried out before Christmas and we had to find another one for the big day.*

—JOHN HAWKINS, *Lenoir*

We decorate our tree with hand-made ornaments collected over three decades.

—MARY JOHN LITTLE RESCH
*Siler City*

When John and I married 32 years ago I began making handmade Christmas tree ornaments. We were very poor since we were both in school and living on our combined incomes of $300 per month. Each year I would select a different theme. I made all the characters from the Wizard of Oz and Cinderella. My objective was to have something unique to hand down to our children as they married and had children of their own. It makes for a very interesting tree, and I can show my grand-daughters orna-ments that their Mom made when she was a little girl.

**—ELLEN P. HARDY**
*Fayetteville*

*Decorating the tree, always a special occasion*

*St. Nicholas figure hand-painted by Ellen Hardy*

Since 1988, having time to trim a tree is a special event for me! When I do, my tree has only white lights and angels—gifts from more than two hundred readers.

—Author **GLORIA HOUSTON**

Christmas tree at the Burlington/Alamance Historic Museum, Burlington

*We decorate our Christmas tree with ornaments made all from seashells, especially angels.*

— **KELLI MOHEREK**
*Pine Knoll Shores*

*A tradition at our home is hand-made swags, topiaries, and other Christmas arrangements. All the decorations are made from boxwood, dried cockscomb, dried roses, etc., most of which I dry myself.*

— **DIANE MESSICK**
*Winston-Salem*

*Fearrington Inn, Pittsboro*

I love Christmas and plan for it all through the year. I start decorating the day after Thanksgiving and have all the trees ready to light by December 1. This gives me time to really enjoy the holidays and share time with family and friends.

Last year I had eighteen trees—one in every room. Seven of them could be seen from the front of the house. My favorite tree is in the master bedroom. It is a Travel Tree with items from all the places we have visited over the past thirty years. It brings back wonderful memories to decorate this tree.

— **CAROL QUINN,** *Advance*

# The Reid House

Built in 1890 by Dr. and Mrs. Thomas Neely Reid in the town of Matthews, this lovely Queen Anne cottage is now owned by the Matthews Historical Foundation. At Christmas, volunteers lavishly decorate the house. In keeping with tradition, high tea is served at four each afternoon during the holiday season.

*The Reid House, Matthews*

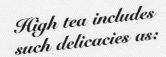

**High tea includes such delicacies as:**

Chocolate Decadence Pound Cake

Applesauce Raisin Spice Bars

Pumpkin Praline Cheesecake

Ginger Cream Scones
with Honey Cinnamon Butter

Chutney Bread
with Lemon Cream Cheese Filling

Sour Cream Parmesan Fans

# Blandwood Mansion

Lovely Blandwood Mansion in downtown Greensboro was once the home of North Carolina Governor John Motley Morehead. Built in the 1790s, it was originally a four-room farmhouse, but Governor Morehead hired noted architect Alexander Jackson Davis to turn it into a stylish Italian villa. Today it has been restored to its mid-1800s splendor, and the public is welcomed during the holiday season. The Christmas Open House features special tours, music, and exhibits.

*OPPOSITE: A colonial doorway decorated with greenery and fresh snow*

*Blandwood Mansion, Greensboro*

LEFT: *Luminaries, Newton*

ABOVE: *The "world's largest living Christmas tree," Wilmington*

RIGHT: *Santa landing at Carolina Beach*

BELOW: *"Christmas Town, USA," McAdenville*

I transform the backyard of my farm

into a fairyland at Christmas.

—ALICE NAYLOR, *Zionville*

*Our whole neighborhood sets out luminaries—paper bags with candles in them. They are weighted down with birdseed and line all the sidewalks and driveways. People in Europe used to believe they were lighting the path for Jesus so he could find his way.*

—JESSIE, *Newton*

*The Oak Hall, Richmond Hill Inn, Asheville*

# Richmond Hill Inn

When Ambassador Richmond Pearson built a beautiful new mansion in Asheville in 1889, he hired noted architect James G. Hill. The focal point of the house was the great Oak Hall, paneled with native oak from surrounding forests. More than a hundred years later, the Oak Hall is still the center of attention during Christmas celebrations at Richmond Hill. A fresh-cut Fraser fir is laden with baroque birdcage ornaments, ribbons, bells, grape clusters, lace flowers, glass balls, and hundreds of twinkling lights.

Commemorating the many great writers associated with the Asheville area, the Richmond Hill Inn has named many of its guest rooms in their honor: poet Sidney Lanier, who camped here before the mansion was built; O'Henry (William Sydney Porter), who is buried in Asheville; novelist, historian, and columnist Wilma Dykeman, the first recipient of the Thomas Wolfe (also from Asheville) Memorial Trophy; novelist Gail Goodwin, who grew up in Asheville where her mother, Kathleen Cole, was a wartime reporter; poet Carl Sandburg, who lived his later years just south of Asheville; and author F. Scott Fitzgerald, who came to Asheville to be near his wife, Zelda, during her stay at a sanitarium.

At Christmas, Richmond Hill guests and the general public are treated to decorations of evergreens, yarrow, and pine cones In addition to beautiful hand-fashioned wreaths, there are dozens of poinsettia plants. Around the tree are antique toys and gifts wrapped much as they would have been in the late 1800s. For the amorous visitor, a "kissing ball" of boxwood and mistletoe is hung in a convenient location.

# EGGNOG CHEESECAKE
*Richmond Hill Inn, Asheville*

## Crust

4 cups fine graham cracker crumbs

2 teaspoons ground cinnamon

6 tablespoons unsalted butter, melted

## Filling

38 ounces cream cheese, softened

1⅛ cups granulated sugar

¼ teaspoon salt

3 large eggs

1 teaspoon ground nutmeg

1 vanilla bean, split; reserve seeds

1¾ cups sour cream

*The biggest treat was to go to Asheville at Christmastime.*

—**SUDIE WHEELER**, *Weaverville*

*Preheat* oven to 300° F.

*To make the crust:* In a medium bowl, combine graham cracker crumbs and cinnamon. Add butter and mix well. Press the mixture onto the bottom and the sides of a 9-inch springform pan and bake for 10 minutes. Chill.

*To make the filling:* In a large bowl, beat cream cheese with an electric mixer on medium speed for 2 minutes or until smooth. Slowly beat in sugar and salt. Add eggs, one at a time, beating well after each egg. Add nutmeg and vanilla seeds and mix well. Blend in sour cream.

*Spread* the filling into the chilled crust. Place the cheesecake in the oven and put a baking pan of hot water on the oven rack below the cheesecake. Bake for 1 hour 20 minutes, or until almost set and a tester inserted in the center comes out clean.

*Loosen* the cheesecake from the pan by running a knife around the inside edge. Let cool in the pan for 30 minutes at room temperature, and then chill in the pan for 6 to 8 hours. Remove from pan and serve chilled or at room temperature. Yields 8 to 10 servings.

*The Theodore Roosevelt Room, Richmond Hill Inn*

# MOTHER'S SUGAR COOKIES

| | |
|---|---|
| 2 cups powdered sugar | 1 teaspoon baking powder |
| 2 sticks butter, softened | 1 teaspoon cream of tartar |
| 2½ cups flour | 1 teaspoon vanilla |
| 1 large egg | ¼ teaspoon salt |

*Preheat* oven to 375° F.

*Beat* sugar and butter for 5 minutes until smooth. Add remaining ingredients and mix thoroughly. Chill dough.

*Cut* chilled dough into four segments. Warm dough slightly with your hands to make it more pliable. Roll the dough out on a floured board or pastry cloth, and cut cookies with cookie cutters.

*Bake* for 5 to 8 minutes, until edges are brown. Makes 2½ dozen cookies.

—**SHIRLEY YOUNT,** *Hickory*

*Mother was known in Conover for her delicious Christmas cookies which she shared with friends, neighbors, grandchildren, service people, one and all. This recipe is an old one from her mother. She made dozens upon dozens, and often we'd still be delivering her Christmas cookies into January to be sure no one was forgotten.*

—**SHIRLEY YOUNT,** *Hickory*

# JOY'S CRAZY CHRISTMAS COOKIES

| | |
|---|---|
| 1½ cup raisins, stewed in water (save water for use in recipe) | ½ teaspoon each ground cloves, nutmeg, and allspice |
| 2 sticks butter, softened | 5 cups raw oats |
| 1½ cup brown sugar | 3 very ripe bananas, mashed |
| ½ cup sugar | 1 cup chopped nuts (walnuts and pecans) |
| 3 eggs | 1 cup diced candied fruit |
| 1 cup whole wheat flour | 1 cup grated coconut |
| 1 cup unbleached flour | grated rind of 1 orange |
| 2 teaspoons cinnamon | ¼ cup orange juice |
| 2 teaspoons salt | 3 teaspoons vanilla |
| 1 teaspoon ground ginger | |
| 1 rounded teaspoon baking soda | |

*Preheat* oven to 350° F.

*In a saucepan,* cover the raisins with water and simmer until plump.

*Cream* butter and both sugars in large mixing bowl. Add eggs and mix well.

*Sift* together dry ingredients and stir in raw oats. Mix into creamed sugar and butter. Add remaining ingredients.

*Drop* teaspoonfuls of batter onto greased cookie sheets, or pour batter into pans to cut into bars. Bake on top rack for 15 to 20 minutes, until lightly brown on top.

—**JOY MINTON,** *Asheville*

*Gingerbread house, Grove Park Inn, Asheville*

## CHRISTMAS ROCKS

1 cup butter or margarine

1 ½ cup sugar

3 eggs

3 cups flour

1 tablespoon cocoa

1 teaspoon each cinnamon,
 mace and nutmeg

½ teaspoon each ginger and allspice

¾ teaspoon baking soda

1 pound pecans

1 pound mixed candied fruit

½ cup currants

¼ cup candied cherries

1 tablespoon liquid coffee

apple and orange slices

*Preheat* oven to 325° F.

*Cream* butter and sugar together until fluffy.

*Beat* eggs until foamy and add to mixture.

*Sift* flour with cocoa, spices and baking soda, and add to creamed sugar a little at a time, mixing thoroughly.

*Mix* all candied fruits and nuts together and dredge with a small amount of flour saved out for this purpose. Add to batter, along with coffee, and mix well.

*Drop* batter by teaspoonfuls onto a greased cookie sheet; not too close together.

*Bake* for 12 to 18 minutes, until a biscuit color. Let cool. Cut an apple and an orange into thin slices and press a slice of fruit onto each rock to add flavor.

*Store* tightly in tins or jars. The longer they stand the better they taste.

—**MARIE B. HOGAN,** *Lenoir*

*My family always expects Christmas Rocks—they're part of our holiday tradition.*

—**MARIE B. HOGAN,** *Lenoir*

## TATER CANDY

1 medium potato

2 boxes powdered sugar

peanut butter

*Cook,* peel, and mash the potato. Add sugar a little at a time until dough thickens so much you can't stir it any longer.

*Take* a handful of dough and roll it out. Spread peanut butter over the dough— as thick as you want. Roll up both ends to make a log. Cool and slice. The dough can be made in advance and frozen.

—**NETTIE HOWELL AND CHARLOTTE HARTLEY,** *Lenoir*

*Every Christmas we make Tater Candy. It's a candy made from Irish potatoes, powdered sugar, and peanut butter, and we give it to all our friends and relatives. Right after Thanksgiving, people start asking, "Are we going to get Tater Candy this year?"*

—**NETTIE HOWELL,** *Lenoir*

When it snows around Christmas, we always make snow
cream. By the time we add the sugar, milk, and food
coloring, we have nothing more than thinned milk with a
strange color, but we think it's the best thing in the world.

—ANONYMOUS, *Enka*

## REFRIGERATOR FRUITCAKE

1 pound pecans

1 pound English walnuts

1 pound raisins

1 pound candied fruit

1 pound marshmallows

1 large can evaporated milk

1 pound graham crackers

*Mix* first four ingredients together and set aside.

*Dissolve* marshmallows in milk over low heat in large saucepan, stirring frequently. Add crushed graham crackers and stir until moistened. Add nuts and fruits and mix.

*Divide* into 3 or 4 loaf-shaped portions and wrap in plastic wrap. Store in refrigerator 2 to 3 days before serving.

—**DR. AND MRS. CHARLES E. CORDELL,** *Asheville*

*I remember Mother cooking for the great day—fruitcakes, pies, a big fat hen, good dressing and so much more.*

—**HENRY LATHAN,** *Hudson*

---

### I Saved my Cake for Santa Claus

*I saved my cake for Santa Claus*
*One Christmas Eve at tea.*
*For if riding makes one hungry*
*How hungry he must be.*
*I put it on the chimney shelf*
*Where he'd be sure to go.*
*I think it does a person good*
*To be remembered so.*
*When everyone was asleep in bed*
*Everyone but me,*
*I tiptoed into Mama's room*
*To see if he had been there yet.*
*Dearie me, it made my feelings ache,*
*There sat a miserable little mouse*
*Eating Santa's cake!*

—**PAULINA BARNEY,** *Advance*
Memorized by Paulina, now 97,
when she was a little girl

---

## SHIRLEY'S LAINE CAKE

Prepare a Duncan Hines White Cake mix according to package directions and bake in four layers instead of three (325° F. for 15 to 20 minutes).

¾ cup butter

4 whole eggs, plus egg yolks
  leftover from cake mix

1 ¾ cups sugar

pinch of salt

¼ to ⅓ cup good bourbon

¾ cup chopped pecans

1 4-ounce carton candied cherries

1 8-ounce carton mixed citrus fruit

2 cartons whipping cream

1 ½ cups flaked coconut

*Cook* butter, whole eggs, egg yolks, sugar and salt in a double boiler until translucent.

*Let cool* and then add bourbon, pecans, cherries and mixed fruit.

*Spread* cooled mixture between layers of cake.

*Whip* cream until stiff, then add 1 cup coconut. Frost cake and sprinkle remaining coconut on top.

—**SHIRLEY YOUNT,** *Hickory*

## FRUIT DIP

1 16-ounce jar marshmallow cream

1 large package of cream cheese

1 teaspoon lemon juice

Stir well and use as a dip for strawberries, grapes and apple slices.

—**ELIZABETH BRUTON,** *Hickory*

# Aunt Trula's Christmas Cake

1 pound butter

2 cups sugar

6 eggs

2 teaspoons lemon flavoring

1 pound white raisins

1 pound pecans or walnuts

4 cups sifted flour

*Preheat* oven to 300° F.

*Cream* butter and sugar and beat until light and fluffy. Add eggs one at a time, beating thoroughly. Mix in lemon flavoring.

*Dredge* raisins and nuts in 1 cup flour and add to creamed sugar. Mix in remaining flour and pour into greased and floured tube pan.

*Bake* 1 hour and 45 minutes.

—**Jane Pruden**, *Asheville*

*Christmas dinner was a wonderful affair because all the aunts brought our favorite foods. It almost became a contest as to which one could please us most. One who did please us greatly was Aunt Trula with her Christmas cake.*

—**Jane Pruden**, *Asheville*

# Chocolate Igloo

1 tablespoon gelatin

¼ cup cold water

⅔ cup sugar

¼ teaspoon salt

1¾ cups milk

1 package German sweet chocolate

3 slightly beaten egg yolks

1 teaspoon vanilla

3 egg whites

1 package devil's food cake mix

1 cup whipping cream

chocolate curls for garnish

*Soften* gelatin in cold water. Combine ⅓ cup sugar, salt and milk in medium saucepan. Add German chocolate and cook over medium heat, stirring constantly, until chocolate is completely melted. Blend mixture well with eggbeater.

*Add* small amount of hot mixture to egg yolks, stirring vigorously. Gradually add remaining hot mixture, stirring constantly. Return to saucepan and cook over low heat until mixture thickens slightly, about 5 minutes. Remove from heat. Add softened gelatin and stir until dissolved. Pour into a large bowl (to use as a mold for the igloo shape) and chill until slightly thickened. Stir in vanilla.

*Beat* egg whites until foamy. Add remaining sugar, 2 tablespoons at a time, and continue beating just until stiff peaks form. Fold into chilled chocolate mixture. Spoon into a 1½-quart mixing bowl and chill until firm, about 2½ hours.

*Prepare* devil's food cake mix. Cool. Freeze one layer for future use.

*Loosen* mold at top edge with sharp knife. Place in bowl of warm water for a few seconds. Remove from water and shake bowl gently to loosen. Place one edge of the bowl 1 inch in from edge of cake layer and unmold on cake. Spread whipped cream over mold and cake. Garnish with chocolate curls.

*Makes* 10 to 12 servings.

—**Naomi Willis**, *Asheville*

# TO GRANNY'S HOUSE WE WENT

There was always one sure way of knowing Christmas was on the way when I was a child growing up in Caldwell County. There were five children in my family, and we knew winter was around the corner because all the meats were in the meat house curing, every jar was full of every imaginable fruit and vegetable, and piles of coal and wood were next to the house.

Granny lived within walking distance of our home. (Back then, walking distance meant within several miles.) Oh, how I loved my Granny and all the times we shared together. I thought she was the smartest woman in the world. She could take nothing and make something beautiful out of it. Even today I can almost smell the goodies from her kitchen.

When the black walnuts started falling, off she would go to the woods. She would gather the nuts and let the green skins dry, and then she put them in Grandpa's old tool shed out back of the house. We used to try to slip in and sneak a few, but she would catch us every time. You simply did *not* mess with Granny's walnuts.

Every Christmas she baked her famous black walnut cake. I don't know how old the recipe is or where it came from, but I do remember the little piece of worn yellow paper she dug out of her kitchen drawer every year at Christmas.

I will always remember Granny standing in the kitchen with a twinkle in her eye and a big smile on her face as she served her special cake. My sister and I still bake the cakes at Christmas. It has become a tradition with our families, just like it was with Granny.

—**PATRICIA HOUCK WOODS**
*Patterson*

## GRANNY McLEAN'S BLACK WALNUT POUND CAKE

*This recipe was torn from an old newspaper over a hundred years old.*

2 sticks butter, softened
½ cup butter-flavored Crisco
3 cups sugar
5 large eggs, room temperature
4 cups plain flour

½ teaspoon baking powder
2 teaspoons black walnut flavoring
1 cup milk
1 cup black walnuts (more if desired)

*Preheat* oven to 325° F.

*Cream* butter and Crisco together with sugar. Beat in eggs one at a time.

*Mix* flour with baking powder. Add flavoring to milk. Toss 2 tablespoons flour with the walnuts and set aside.

*Alternate* flour and milk with the creamed mixture. When batter is well mixed, fold in walnuts. Pour batter into a greased and floured tube pan.

*Bake* 1½ hours.

—**PATRICIA HOUCK WOODS**, *Patterson*

*I grew up in Wilkes County and we used to go "Santa Clausing" at Christmas. It was a lot like Trick or Treat, and neighbors would give us candy. If they didn't, we would trick them by taking their corn shucks.*

—**GWENDA HAYES HOLADAY**
*Boone*

# CRANBERRY POUND CAKE

*Cake*

2 cups cranberries, washed and dried, at room temperature

3 cups flour

1 teaspoon baking powder

½ teaspoon salt

2 sticks butter, softened

2 cups sugar

5 eggs, room temperature

2 tablespoons Grand Marnier

grated zest of 1 orange

*Glaze*

1 cup confectioners sugar

2 tablespoons orange juice

1 teaspoon Grand Marnier

*"In hope that St. Nicholas soon would be there..."*

**Preheat** oven to 325° F

**Toss** berries with ¼ cup flour and set aside. Sift remaining flour with baking powder and salt and set aside.

**In mixer,** cream butter and sugar. Add eggs one at a time, beating well after each one. Add Grand Marnier and orange zest and beat until fluffy. Fold flour into batter until well blended. Gently stir in berries. Pour into greased and floured 10-inch tube or bundt pan.

**Bake** 1 hour and 15 minutes or until cake tests done. Cool for 10 minutes before removing from pan.

**Whisk** confectioners sugar, orange juice and Grand Marnier until smooth and pour over cake after it has cooked completely. Allow glaze to harden before slicing cake.

—**MARY JOHN LITTLE RESCH,** *Siler City*

# CHOCOLATE NO-BAKE

½ cup butter

½ cup milk

2 cups sugar

¼ cup (or less) cocoa

½ cup peanut butter

1 ½ teaspoons vanilla

3 ¼ cups uncooked oatmeal

**Heat** butter and milk. Add sugar and cocoa, and boil for 5 minutes, stirring constantly. Add peanut butter, vanilla and oats. Stir until blended.

**Drop** by teaspoons on waxed paper. Let stand 30 minutes.

—**VICKIE LONG,** *Yadkinville*

The women in my family like to begin the Christmas holiday by baking cookies together. There are four generations in my kitchen working on those cookies! We give a few simple gifts to Mama and the great granddaughter to set the mood, and we play Christmas carols while we work. We usually fix a pot of soup and then the whole family eats supper together and samples the cookies. This is how we get in the holiday spirit—getting together and spending time with each other, which is the best part.

—**VICKIE LONG,** *Yadkinville*

# THE ONE AND ONLY CHRISTMAS GIFT

The home where I grew up was not decorated with luxuries or hanging chandeliers. There were no carpeted floors or fine furniture carved from oak or pine. There were no fancy beds when our eyes became heavy with sleep, only handmade quilts and plain mattresses, which served us just as well.

Christmas was as simple as the house we lived in. We never had a store-bought tree. We cut our Christmas tree from the fields around our little country home and then decorated it with the few decorations we had, which were mostly handmade ornaments crafted from our own imaginations. But our tree was as pretty to us as the most elaborate ones around.

Underneath were no shiny packages tied with glittery bows. Frankly, almost always it was bare except for the cotton wrapped around the bottom of the tree. We were lucky if there were gifts at all because we were a family of eleven children, which explains it all. Our family's small income was used to keep a roof over our heads, food on the table, and clothes on our backs.

The kitchen was as modest as all the other rooms in our house, but at Christmas it seemed brighter, warmer, and more inviting. Mom always cooked something a little extra special on Christmas. She would bake pies from apples that she had preserved for winter. She would make sweet potato custards and her famous Christmas cake. Mom was a wonderful cook!

We would all sit down together at the kitchen table and enjoy our Christmas dinner, which was cooked in cast iron pots and pans, then served to us on mis-matched plates, glasses, and flatware. But our meal was just as delicious as food served on the finest china and silver.

I always thought of our traditional Christmas dinner as Mom's special gift to each of us. For it truly was made with each of us in mind, served without partiality through the goodness of her heart. And each one of us truly did go away from the table satisfied. I realize now that all Christmas gifts aren't placed under a tree, because we received our one and only Christmas gift around the kitchen table, served with a mother's love—which was the wrapping with a pretty bow.

—LILLIAN P. SIMPSON, *Cherryville*

# CHERRY-NUT CAKE

*A family Christmas favorite for more than fifty years*

1 cup butter

2 cups sugar

4 eggs

3 cups sifted flour

2 teaspoons baking powder

pinch of salt

⅓ cup evaporated milk, undiluted

1 16-ounce jar maraschino cherries, chopped

⅓ cup maraschino cherry juice

2 cups chopped pecans

*Preheat* oven to 325° F.

*Cream* butter and sugar. Add eggs one at a time, beating well after each one.

*Sift* 2 cups flour with baking powder and salt. Alternately add flour and milk to the creamed mixture. Use the remaining cup of flour to dredge the nuts. Add nuts and cherries, including cherry juice, to batter.

*Bake* in greased and floured tube pan for at least 1 hour or until done.

—**MARY ELDER**, *Banner Elk*

# LEMON POUND CAKE

*Cake*

2 sticks butter

½ cup plain Crisco or butter-flavored

3 cups sugar

6 eggs

6 tablespoons lemon juice

1 tablespoon lemon peelings

1 teaspoon vanilla

1 teaspoon lemon flavoring

3 cups flour

1 teaspoon baking powder

½ teaspoon salt

1 cup milk

*Lemon Icing*

2 cups powdered sugar

1 tablespoon lemon peels, grated

3 to 4 tablespoons lemon juice

*Preheat* oven to 325° F.

*Cream* butter, Crisco and sugar until fluffy. Add eggs one at a time and beat well. Add lemon juice, lemon peelings, vanilla and lemon flavoring.

*Sift* together flour, baking powder and salt, and add to creamed mixture, alternating with flour and milk. Blend well.

*Spoon* batter into a greased and floured 10-inch bundt pan.

*Bake* for 1 hour and 15 minutes or until toothpick comes out clean.

*Make icing* by creaming powdered sugar, grated lemon peels and lemon juice until smooth. Drizzle icing over warm cake.

—**NAOMI A. SIMMONS**, *Winston-Salem*

## COCONUT ATTIC CAKE

2 sticks margarine, whipped

½ cup Crisco

2 ¾ cups sugar

2 teaspoons vanilla

5 eggs

1 cup sweet milk

3 cups sifted plain flour

¾ teaspoon salt

½ teaspoon baking powder

1 ½ pints whipping cream (whipped)

grated coconut

*Preheat* oven to 350° F.

*Cream* margarine, Crisco, sugar and vanilla together. Add beaten eggs and milk.

*Sift* dry ingredients together and mix slowly into creamed mixture.

*Pour* into three 9-inch greased and floured cake pans and bake for 30 minutes. Cool.

*Spread* whipped cream on each layer and grated coconut on top of each of these.

—**Clarice D. Lopp,** *Thomasville*

*Attic Cake has been a holiday tradition in our family for many years. The grandchildren always expected fresh coconut cake with whipped cream icing. During the holiday season, the refrigerator was always filled with food of all sorts and there was no room for the cake. So the disappearing stairway would be lowered and the coconut cake placed in the cold attic. Hence the name Attic Cake.*

—**The Doug Lopp Family**

*Thomasville*

## PECAN PIE

1 cup dark Karo syrup

½ cup white sugar

½ stick of butter

1 teaspoon vanilla

3 eggs

1 ½ cups chopped pecans

9-inch pie shell (uncooked)

*Preheat* oven to 450° F.

*Cook* the Karo syrup, sugar, butter and vanilla until dissolved.

*Beat* eggs in a mixing bowl, gradually adding the hot syrup to eggs while beating. Add pecans. Pour mixture into pie shell.

*Bake* for 10 minutes at 450° F. and then for 35 minutes at 350° F.

—**Kathryn Humphries,** *Asheville*

*Each Christmas we select a family that is in need and help make Christmas a little brighter and happier. We make candy and cookies and deliver them to the shut-in and elderly.*

—**Patricia Houck Woods**

*Patterson*

## COLONIAL PUMPKIN PIE

1 ½ cups cooked pumpkin

1 cup brown sugar

½ teaspoon salt

1 teaspoon each cinnamon and ginger

⅛ teaspoon allspice

2 tablespoons molasses

3 eggs, slightly beaten

1 cup evaporated milk

9-inch deep-dish pie shell (uncooked)

*Preheat* oven to 425° F.

*Combine* first seven ingredients. Add eggs and milk, and mix thoroughly. Pour into pie shell.

*Bake* for 40 to 45 minutes.

—**Esther Harmon,** *Banner Elk*

*Sledding in Hickory*

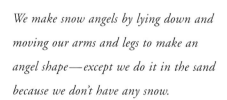

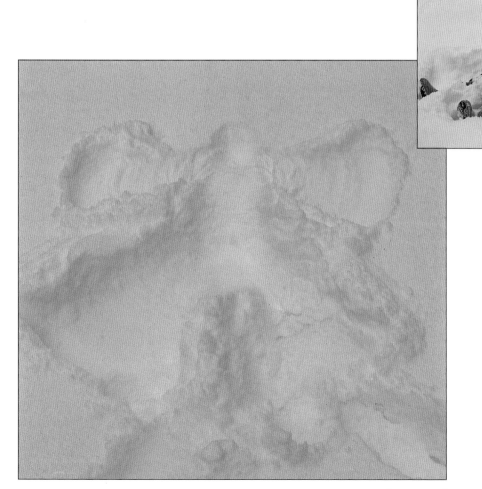

*We make snow angels by lying down and moving our arms and legs to make an angel shape—except we do it in the sand because we don't have any snow.*

**—KELLI MOHEREK**
*Pine Knoll Shores*

*Snow angel*

*Tryon Palace at Christmas, New Bern*

# Tryon Palace

"The opening of the [Palace], together with the King's Birthday, were celebrated here on Wednesday last….In the Evening his Excellency gave a very grand and noble Entertainment and Ball…." This report of festivities was written in December of 1770, when Tryon Palace in New Bern was opened for Royal Governor William Tryon and his family. North Carolina was still a British colony, and the birthday to which the quote refers was not that of Christ, the King, but rather of England's King George III.

The Tryon family most likely celebrated Christmas in the Old English tradition, on the twelve days from December 25 to January 6. This would include dinners, balls, visiting, and, most of all, church gatherings. Children in the colonies were likely to receive religious books as New Year's gifts during the celebrations. Decorations consisted primarily of greenery dressing the home.

Today, the Tryon Palace Historic Sites and Gardens are a triumph of historic restoration. In addition to the palace, there are five other restored buildings.

*Eighteenth-century style dancing, Tryon Palace*

In the 1780s, New Bern's John Wright Stanly House was home to the wealthy family of a shipbuilder. It is decorated for the holidays with a rustic simplicity. Dating from the 1830s, the Dixon–Stevenson House is decorated much more festively. Children probably received cakes, fruits, nuts, candy, or coins at Christmas.

From 1862 to 1864 New Bern celebrated Christmas as a Union-occupied city. In winter quarters,

Union soldiers spent their days reading and writing letters. They were grateful for Christmas gifts of food and warm clothing, and attempted to bring homelike touches to their surroundings.

In the late nineteenth century, children in the New Bern Academy looked forward to a special treat—a decorated Christmas tree. The custom of decorating a tree at Christmas became popular in the U.S. after England's Queen Victoria received a Christmas tree from Prince Albert, her German-born husband. Such trees were actually more common in schools than they were in homes.

*Governor Tryon's library*

The Commission House is decorated in a Victorian style, with candles on the tree and stockings stuffed with toys and candy for good boys and girls—and lumps of coal and switches for naughty children. Visitors touring this building will also notice a 1940s touch, a reminder of when military men and women were stationed nearby during World War II. Longing to be home for the holidays, they would flock trees with whipped soap flakes to make it look like snow, which is still done today.

Tours of the Tryon Palace and the surrounding buildings are popular during the holidays. The most beautiful of all are the candlelight tours of the palace, when more than 800 candles and lanterns light the way for visitors, carolers, dancers, and harpsichord musicians.

*Re-creation of Union
winter quarters*

## WHEN THE ANIMALS TALK

Throughout the South, especially in the Appalachian Mountains, folks pay special attention to their farm animals. According to legend, these creatures gently breathed on the Christ child to keep him warm in the unheated stable, and He rewarded them by allowing them to speak on Christmas Eve. As the clock strikes midnight, the old-timers swear, the animals sink to their knees in worship, facing in the direction of Bethlehem. Many North Carolina mountain people claim to have seen this phenomenon, and some even claim to have heard the animals talk.

*Birthplace of Zebulon Baird Vance, governor of North Carolina from 1862–65 and again from 1877–79, Buncombe County*

# Hope Plantation

While many of North Carolina's great plantations built during the colonial and federal periods have fallen into ruin, Hope Plantation near Windsor managed to survive the passage of time and has been beautifully restored. Constructed in 1803 for Governor David Stone, Hope Plantation was a self-sustaining plantation, with hundreds of people living and working there. It boasted a grist mill, sawmill, blacksmith's shop, and houses for spinning and weaving, although many of these buildings are no longer standing.

In the early days at Hope Plantation, there were probably very few decorations at Christmas, since the idea did not become popular until later in the nineteenth century. With that in mind, volunteers who decorate the buildings for holiday tours and events strive to use all-natural materials.

Festoons of pine and boxwood with pine cones and berries decorate the rooms, along with arrangements of oranges, lemons, and pineapples. The King–Blazemore House, built in 1765, is also located on the Hope Plantation. Representing an even earlier period, this building is very sparsely decorated.

During the Christmas Open House at the Hope Plantation, music fills the air and the delicious smell of cider and cookies creates a feeling of Christmas past. A recent holiday addition is a dessert table in the Drawing Room. The table is stacked with traditional sweets such as plum puddings, sugar cookies, a Great Cake, a Twelfth Night Cake, cones made of raisins and fruits, and cream-filled cones drizzled with sugar called *croque un bouche*, meaning "crackle in the mouth."

Hope Plantation takes on a festive mood at the holidays, and a Christmas visit here offers unique insight into the way a North Carolina plantation operated during the early nineteenth century.

*ABOVE: Basement kitchen at Historic Hope Plantation, Windsor*

*Conestoga wagon at a home near Valle Crucis*

I remember Christmas in the 1920s. We were not rich, but neither were we poor. We were part of the great, wonderful middle class in our country. At home, we had a Montgomery Ward catalog. I would spend hours looking at the toy section. I had to find something special because Santa would only bring one gift. One year, I found it—a wooden toolbox with hammer, saw, other tools, nails, and screws. I sent a letter to Santa at once. On Christmas morning I jumped from my bed and dashed to the hall. There it was under the tree! I had my toolbox. Next, on to the stocking. I had an apple, an orange, a penny-box of raisins, and a few pieces of candy. Santa had really come! All that day I played with my toolbox and showed it to my friends. Christmas night I went to sleep thinking of the great things I could make with my gift!

— **DAVID C. HEAVNER,** Lincolnton

# THE LENOIR TOPIC

## Christmas in Lenoir — 1883

In Lenoir on Christmas Eve of 1883, the deep darkness of the town where no streetlights glimmered, glowed with wavering flickers of gas and candlelight sparkling from the small panes in the old courthouse. The halo around the building standing in the center of town outlined dark ruts of wagon trails winding about the faded red brick building.

Inside a great green Christmas tree, snowy with popcorn chains and paper ornaments, drooped beneath its heavy burden of gifts. Most of the towns 400 villagers were gathered in the hall, heated by a big cast iron stove and the warmth of holiday cheer. Christmas was in everyone's bones. Laughter ran from the courthouse through streets tinkling small silver bells in the frosty air, as beaus and belles and others unwrapped suggestive, funny gifts.

Another Christmas tree program was being held at Powelltown Baptist Church, where a large tree hung weighted with gifts for all the Sunday School.

One was also in progress at Littlejohn's Church where Rev. M. Sherrill and Rev. D.H. Tuttle made talks prior to the cutting down and distributing of gifts by the committee....Good natured jesting and silly gifts were the cause of much merriment. One young man was given a gift of soap, with the following poem attached:
'Tis hope that keeps our spirits up/ 'Tis hope that keeps our mem-ries green/ 'Tis hope that makes our lives sublime/ 'Tis soap that keeps us clean.

Christmas day was a time of family gatherings with loaded tables featuring 'possum pie and potatoes and turkey.

The following week there was a round of festivities, including sociables, Christmas trees, storm parties and quiltings.

The Lenoir Topic reported, "There were several social parties at private residences during the week. Among them we may mention evening parties at Mrs. Ervin's Wednesday night and at Dr. Beall's Thursday night.... On Wednesday night a party of young folks with light hearts and 'fantastic toes' met together and enjoyed a delightful hop at the Central Hotel. Pretty girls from Lenoir and vicinity, pretty girls from 'the river' and pretty girls from Burke danced away the gliding hours and as they danced they broke the hearts of the graces and of the boys.

"These young people on pleasure bent, again on Monday of last week enjoyed a most delight hop at Palmyra, the residence of Mr. S. L. Patterson on the Yakdin...."

Prominent Lenoir men attended a railroad dinner at Hickory on Thursday of Christmas week. Everyone in the area was intensely interested in the progress of the narrow gauge railway construction between Lenoir and Hickory, which was expected to relieve the isolation of Lenoir, separated from the lower country by wide rivers and deep forests.

W.W. Scott Jr., editor of the Topic, concluded the Christmas issue with the following: "The holidays are over, and, having enjoyed them to our bent, it is proper that we should carry happy hearts and sweet dispositions with us through the coming year and that, as we buckle down to the serious affairs of life, we should not look upon our duties as so many crosses and burdens, but should rather regard them in the light of privileges and ourselves as fortunate in being allowed to be the pioneers and up-builders of what is the garden spot of North Carolina. Hail! Eighteen Hundred and Eighty Four and to thee, Oh! Narrow Gauge, Godspeed!"
— by Nancy Alexander, 1933

*Palmyra, near Lenoir, in the 1800s*

# NEWS-TOPIC

## Christmas in Lenoir – 1945

For the first time in five years the people of Lenoir and Caldwell Counties will celebrate the joyous Christmas season without the existence of a devastating war, although with many homes missing the absent service man who has not yet returned from the battle areas.

It is indeed a happy Christmas for the nation that recently emerged victorious from the most threatening war in its existence. The fact that the scourge of conflict did not scar the continental area of this country does not mean that the hand of war was not heavy upon the land nor should we be unmindful of…the fact that in Caldwell County alone there are nearly a hundred homes with a vacant chair symbolizing the utmost in sacrificial service to their country that it may continue to enjoy the blessing peace and freedom. The thoughts and affection of a grateful nation will abide in these homes now and always.

In celebrating the birth of the Prince of Peace the people of the United States exhibit a broad tolerance that makes the occasion a festival for all the people…. The good humor that prevails and kindly sympathy for the unfortunate and the boundless efforts to bring happiness to boys and girls, make the Christmas season appear universal.

The day will be marked as usual, by religious services, the giving of gifts, the exchange of salutation and greetings, the merriment of delighted children and the deep, if less exuberant joy of those of mature years. Altogether it will be a day of unusual happiness for millions of people who for five years have been restrained through anxiety for loved ones on the battle fronts in all parts of the world….

In extending our best wishes for our readers…we must also extend our greetings to the absent men and women of the community who remain overseas. It is hard for them to be away from home and loved ones, now that the war is over, and it is equally disappointed to their loved ones.

At the same time the disappointment should be tempered by the realization that those overseas and in camps at home, serve the cause we celebrate. Without their services and those of others now happily present, the celebration of Christmas would not now assume such splendid proportions.

*—Submitted by* **JOHN HAWKINS,** *columnist, NEWS-TOPIC*

*Battleship* North Carolina *decorated for Christmas*

# Carolina Holiday Humor

Maybe it's the way they were raised, or the weather, or maybe living in the South provides exceptional material. Whatever the reason, North Carolinians seem to know how to laugh. The joy of laughter is often interwoven with the many diverse traditions and celebrations throughout the state. A number of North Carolinian cartoonists have done well on the national scene, often drawing from their Carolina roots to find humor that all of America can appreciate.

## UNPLUGGING THE CHRISTMAS MACHINE

Charlotte cartoonist *Jim Hunt* draws heavily on his experiences as a father for his humor.

© 1996, H. Ketcham Enterprises, Inc.

Artist **Marcus Hamilton** now illustrates *Dennis the Menace* from his studio in Charlotte.

*Cover art by Marcus Hamilton*

The Saturday Evening Post © 1978

*Alley Oop* cartoonist **Dave Graue** of Hendersonville has become well known among friends and family for his Christmas cards.

May your holidays be filled with joy and laughter!

Eliza, Dave, and Dan Graue

*Jim Scancarelli's* Gasoline Alley, created in Charlotte, often reflects familiar North Carolina locations, such as this country church near Elkin.

My New Year's sermon deals with a man who put an ad in the paper...

*Connemara, home of Carl Sandburg, Flat Rock*

# Carl Sandburg's Connemara

Poet Carl Sandburg was in his sixties when he and his family moved to Flat Rock, and he considered his years here as some of the best of his life. Perched high on a hill, Sandburg's house, named Connemara, overlooked his farm and a scenic lake. Life at Connemara was relaxed and pleasant, often including visitors from many parts of the world. In this pastoral setting Sandburg wrote and sang and entertained friends.

In keeping with the Sandburgs' lifestyle, Christmas at Connemara was simple, with a single tree and poinsettias placed throughout the house. A good, hearty meal was served to family and friends, and there was undoubtedly music throughout the day. Sandburg's big, comfortable easy chair is still pulled up next to the piano, with his guitar propped up nearby.

During the holiday season, from the first Saturday after Thanksgiving and every Saturday until Christmas, Connemara is open to the public in the evening. The path to the house is lit by luminaries. When visitors arrive, they are offered hot cider and cookies and are entertained with various programs about Sandburg.

*OPPOSITE: Toy Store, Beech Mountain*

# Toys—North Carolina Mountain Style

Childish laughter mingles with the noise of pecking chickens, dancing feet, and shouts of "gee-haw!" These expressions of happiness are the Christmas sounds of children playing with handmade toys from the mountains of North Carolina.

In Christmases past, children in more affluent homes might have received lace-bedecked dolls or shiny red wagons, but in poor Appalachian homes, those items were expensive luxuries only seen in pictures or store windows. Parents couldn't afford store-bought gifts and instead made toys for their children from pieces of wood, lengths of string, chunks of stone, strips of leather, scraps of fabric, and dried corn shucks.

Traditional Appalachian toys are still made by many mountain families. Luther Ashby of the Pioneer Folk Toys Company in Hudson markets toys handcrafted by family members. "There's still a lot of interest in these toys," he claims. "They're simple, but children—as well as adults —seem to love them as much as they do video games or other, more sophisticated toys."

According to Mr. Ashby, the origin of many of these toys hark back hundreds of years to Scotland, Ireland, and England, as well as other European countries. Emigrants who settled in the Appalachians brought these beloved toys with them when they came to America.

Limber jack, carved from poplar, does a lively mountain buck dance on a board of yellow pine. A flock of chickens pecks at food atop a wooden paddle, the action set in motion by a soapstone weight. Made from mountain laurel, the gee-haw whimmydiddle is most likely of Native American origin. Also known as the hooey stick, this simple toy has a twirling propeller. When given the "gee-haw" command, usually used for horses and mules, the propeller changes direction—if you know the trick, that is.

Many North Carolinians can remember trying to catch a ball in a cup, and those of us who have tried to master the idiot stick can remember feeling quite like idiots. These traditional mountain toys have entertained children for two hundred years, and hopefully they will still be making children laugh for many years to come.

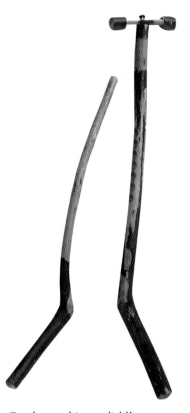

*Gee-haw whimmydiddle*

*Jacob's ladder constantly changes as the colorful blocks unfold*

*We open gifts on Christmas Eve. But first, to calm the children down, we light candles and read the Christmas story from Luke, reminding them of the true meaning of Christmas and why we give each other gifts.*

**—Wrenn Johnson**
*Morehead City*

*Children enjoy a dancing limber jack outside of the General Store at Murray's Mill, near Catawba*

It was a tradition in our family to open one gift on Christmas Eve. That gift was always new pajamas, so we would go to bed on Christmas Eve in brand new pj's.

—**APRIL COX**, Lenoir

*I well remember the very first time it was suggested to me that there just might not be a Santa Claus. On Christmas Day when I was about six or seven, my three girl cousins and I were sitting in my uncle's old Chevrolet sedan in the warm sunshine. One cousin announced with some importance, "Ain't no Santa, you know!" Talk about some upset children! As I recall, the argument was not settled that day, but the seed of doubt was planted and we discussed it furiously among our little selves.*

—**JUDGE OLIVER NOBLE**, *Pink Hill*

*There's something about chocolate-covered cherries and the Christmas season that go together.*

—**JOHN HAWKINS,** *Lenoir*

*The only way we had to heat the house was a fireplace and wood cook stove. Daddy liked to tease us about Santa coming down the chimney. On Christmas Eve he would tell us that he was going to light a big fire right before bedtime and Santa wouldn't get to come down and leave our gifts; but he always did. Oh to bring all those wonderful times back.*

—**THELMA BEASLEY GEORGE**
*Westfield*

*Our favorite tradition is opening gag gifts on Christmas Eve. Gag gifts are the center of our celebration.*

—**GLORIA HOUSTON**

*Gifts were simple and inexpensive, but I remember my grandmother always giving each of us girls a handkerchief.*

—**JANE PRUDEN,** *Asheville*

# THE YEAR THE REINDEER SNEEZED

It was Christmas Eve and Santa was about halfway done delivering gifts to children around the world. Up till now he had been ahead of schedule, but he began to notice the reindeer were getting jumpy. It was usually easy to guide the reindeer because Rudolph was such an excellent leader, but that night something was definitely wrong. Rudolph's nose began to blink rapidly, like a brilliant red strobe light.

Santa called out to Rudolph to slow down, but his voice was drowned out by the sound of sneezing. First one, then two, then all the reindeer began sneezing and twitching. Poor Santa lost control of the sleigh as the reindeer sneezed and snorted themselves into a tizzy. Instead of gliding along smoothly as they were trained to do, the reindeer fumbled and bumped heads as their eyes crossed. Poor Santa was bounced and knocked from side to side in the sleigh, and the beautifully wrapped packages were falling out of his sack. The only thing to do was for Santa to land and find out what had gone wrong. It was going to delay the delivery but it had to be done.

Santa checked his map and found out they had landed in a drop zone at Fort Bragg, North Carolina. The moon was bright, giving him enough light to see the miles and miles of pine trees. He took the harnesses off the reindeer and began rubbing their backs until they stopped sneezing. The poor things were dazed. He remembered that Mrs. Claus had washed the harnesses just before they left for their long trip. Perhaps that new detergent had caused an allergic reaction in the reindeer.

When he looked up, in the direction of the herd, he saw no herd! The reindeer had wandered off into the trees. He could hear them running, giggling, and playing in the pine trees. Oh no, he thought, now what was he going to do?

Just about then, Santa saw the military police pull up. "Hey, what's going on here?" the MP called out as he flashed a light on Santa. Well, word traveled fast at Fort Bragg and Pope Air Force Base and in the town of Fayetteville, and within minutes thousands of people were in their cars heading to the drop zone to help Santa find the missing reindeer.

What a glorious sight to see so many people show up to help. What wonderful people! Santa thought. The military set up base stations and bonfires were built. Families and soldiers and airmen all gathered with thousands of flashlights to light up the area. You could hear Christmas carols being sung, and laughter and joy filled the air.

*Old-fashioned sleigh,*
*Beech Mountain*

It only took a few hours to find all the reindeer and corral them. Some soldiers rigged up a sturdy harness. Santa gave the itchy harness to the General for safe keeping. Actually Santa didn't want the reindeer to get near it for fear they'd start sneezing again.

With the reindeer harnessed, fed, and rested, Santa was ready to resume his famous Christmas Eve delivery trip. Tears of gratitude were in his eyes as he boarded his sleigh and waved goodbye to the people. He left them all a very special gift, a gift they would remember for the rest of their lives.

On Christmas morning. Fort Bragg, Pope Air Force Base, and Fayetteville woke up and felt something was different. Last night—was it a dream? Did it really happen? No one could quite put a finger on it, but something was definitely different—families were closer, friends reached out to each other, old hurts were healed, loneliness was gone, and the spirit of love was everywhere.

As for Santa's gift—well, Christmas is just so much more festive with snow, and snow it did. All of North Carolina was blanketed in the most beautiful covering of pure, white, fluffy snow for Christmas day!

—**JEANETTE E. MORTON,** *Fayetteville*

*Every year we purchase and date a new book pertaining to Christmas. We plan on dividing the books between the children when they marry.*

—**DEBBIE PAISLEY,** *Morganton*

*We leave all our guests a little Christmas present on their pillow at Christmas. As innkeepers, Christmas for us is one giant house party.*

—**JENNIFER AND JEREMY WAINWRIGHT**
Pine Crest Inn, Tryon

*We finish our Christmas shopping early so we can go to the mall and watch people. We sit for hours and have the best time.*

—**DAVID AND SUSAN GUEST**
*Hickory*

North Carolina writers have given us many Christmas
stories, such as O'Henry's "The Gift of the Magi" and
Gloria Houston's "The Year of the Perfect Christmas Tree"

My mother always read "The Night Before
Christmas" to us on Christmas Eve before we
went to bed.

— **BILL PITTMAN**, *Wilson*

*Pinkerton of Lenoir, dressed for the holidays*

*Toy train in Santa's village, Newton*

*Lena Bengtson*

*Lena Bengtson*

Of Swedish descent, North Carolinian Lena Bengtson has been practicing the art of "silhouette cutting" for more than twenty years. She primarily makes portraits of children, but also of animals, adults, and even angels. It is common for families in North Carolina to have their children's portraits cut every year at Christmas and collect them as a series.

*Christmas Day, meant lots of company. Aunt Bertha and Uncle Davis always brought a present. I liked the smell of his cigar smoke. Pa Bill had a peppermint cane for all the children and sometimes he used his pocketknife to break off pieces for the little ones. Grown-up folks sat around the fire, talking mainly. We children ran and played with our new toys. Dinner was at the long table with benches. Uncle John Good would ask the blessing. My, how time flew and soon the day was over. Folks left, going back home before dark. The day was about over and we were trying real hard to hold onto that good feeling, and then we realized that the feeling wouldn't go away in a day. It would remain with us as long as we thought of Christmas.*

—**HENRY LATHAN,** *Hudson*

*A shiny Radio Flyer filled with toys—a Christmas dream come true*

For many years our family put together a puzzle on Christmas Day. We kept working on it until it was done, even if it took several days.

**—ROBERT KRAAY,** Hickory

Seven shoeboxes with names written on them were placed near the fireside on Christmas Eve. Going to bed early and trying hard to fall asleep wasn't always easy. Then we were up bright and early to see what Santa brought. My shoebox held a world of delight. I remember one Christmas, when all the children together got a red wagon—a Radio Flyer.

**—HENRY LATHAN,** Hudson

# A FAMILY CHRISTMAS

Christmas 1967 was particularly special for me. My father had abandoned me and my mother several years earlier and it had been hard on her. Then she renewed an old friendship with a man who had lost his wife. He had four kids, all younger than me, and he worked in another state, so the kids came to live with us. I must admit I resented these strangers invading my home and sharing my mother's attention. Well, Christmas rolled around and we all wanted bikes. Money was tight so we never dreamed we might all get bikes, but we were hoping. Christmas morning came and we gathered at the top of the stairs. Someone suggested we all hold hands, which we did from the top of the stairs to the living room. There they were—five gleaming bikes, five different sizes. That day marked the beginning of us becoming a family.

—**KNIGHT CHAMBERLAIN,** *Lumberton*

*One year Moma asked what we wanted for Christmas. My brother asked for a BB gun and I for a camera. Come Christmas they were under the tree. Grandma said taking pictures was the workings of the Devil and the Lord gave us all good memories so we wouldn't need the workings of the Devil. Well, my camera was special and from then on I took pictures of all the family get-togethers. Years passed, and in 1969 Hurricane Camille took my high school yearbooks and photo albums. Then Hurricane Hugo stripped me of the rest of my pictures. Grandma was right—material things will never matter as much as family, home, friends, and memories.*

—**BERNICE L. COUCH**

*Winston-Salem*

*My thoughts go back to the late thirties and early forties. About a month before Christmas we would get very excited, even though we knew Santa wouldn't bring us very much. Times were hard and Mama and Daddy farmed. Tobacco was our money crop. Before Christmas we would get a catalog from Sears and Roebuck. We would tell Mama all the things we wanted and would get a few. I would usually get a doll, a tea set, orange slice candy, an orange or two, chocolate drops, and nuts. I remember one Christmas I got a little table and chairs. My dolls and I had a lot of tea parties. Another Christmas my doll was so ugly I cried. I still have that doll and most of the others too.*

—**THELMA BEASLEY GEORGE,** *Westfield*

*The Biltmore House, Asheville*

# Christmas at Biltmore Estate

Five train cars pulled into the small train depot in Biltmore Village a few days prior to Christmas in 1895. Aboard the train were family and friends from New York and Newport,

eagerly awaiting their first look at George Vanderbilt's newly constructed 250-room chateau, adorned, in anticipation of company, with more holiday cheer than they ever imagined.

The merriment of Christmas day was shared by all who attended and even by those who caught a brief glimpse through the local newspaper, the Asheville Citizen:

*George Vanderbilt*

*The hearth fires on Biltmore House cracked a cheery Christmas warming to members of George W. Vanderbilt's family who came from the North to honor the occasion. Apart from the pleasure of a family gathering on the day of the great festival of the year, the event of absorbing interest on the estate was the welcome given in the great house to the resident workman, wives and children.... The hour of the festivities was put on at 11 o'clock and upward of 200 persons were promptly present in the Banquet Hall when Mr. Vanderbilt in a short speech wished the company a merry Christmas....A beautiful tree that stood in the Banquet Hall causing the liveliest anticipation of the little folks, was then stripped of its heavy trimmings of gifts. Each of the guests was remembered.*

And even The New York Times took note of the celebration that day:

*A Christmas tree donation was given at 11 o'clock today to all employees on the estate. Barrels of mistletoe, wagonloads of holly and cartloads of packages were distributed. A dinner was later served to the employees.*

*The company now at Biltmore is made up exclusively of members of the Vanderbilt family, but the festivities will broaden toward the close of the week, when a large company of Mr. Vanderbilt's New York friends will be his guests for, perhaps, ten days. The time will be spent in coaching parties, hunting, fox chasing, quail shooting and fishing.*

A century later, guests still look forward to glimpses of the Christmas season at America's largest home, Biltmore House, and what it was like for the Vanderbilts that first December. And because the house and its contents have been carefully preserved to reflect how it was in George Vanderbilt's day, visitors can easily imagine themselves as participants in a turn-of-the-century holiday celebration.

Vanderbilt traditions, such as the towering forty-foot Banquet Hall tree adorned with brightly papered packages, still continue today over 200,000 guests that visit Biltmore Estate during its Christmas season, mid-November through December. Elegant decorations are found in all rooms that are open to the public (over one-third of the house), including the kitchens, servants quarters, and even the bowling alley.

The first floor sparkles with four 14-foot Christmas trees in the Tapestry Gallery, each decorated with Biltmore's own collection of German hand-blown glass ornaments. The Winter Garden overflows with colorful poinsettias grown in the Estate's greenhouses. A trip up the spiraling 102-step Grand Staircase wrapped with fresh garland leads visitors to a charming display of Victorian toys under the tree in the Second Floor Living Hall. And on the basement level, a handmade gingerbread replica of Biltmore House in the Main Kitchen delights every guest.

*Forty-foot Christmas tree in the Great Banquet Hall*

To make all of this possible, the floral staff starts preparing for each Christmas season a year in advance. Cathy Barnhardt, floral designer at Biltmore Estate for the last 18 years, uses archival records and period literature to re-create the elegance of Christmas during the Gilded Age. She uses a variety of materials, from live wreaths made by the landscaping staff to hand-blown German glass ornaments, to obtain the look that continues to thrill guests at the Estate.

Over thirty-five trees are decorated throughout the house, each reflecting the mood of its beautiful surroundings. Color, texture and even purpose of a room often dictate what the Christmas tree will look like. Barnhardt makes a point to change the decorations each season because so many guests return from year to year. Other holiday decorating supplies include over 200 wreaths, 2,000 poinsettias, 600 hand-tied bows, and nearly 21,000 feet of evergreen roping.

*The Biltmore House Library in holiday splendor*

During the season, the house is filled with familiar holiday tunes from live performances in the House by the area's most talented performers. All tours are self-directed, so guests are encouraged to pause and enjoy the Christmas music. Because the Estate has eight specialty gift shops, guests often bring the sights and sounds of the Biltmore House into their own homes for the holidays. Tours of the Biltmore Estate Winery, the most visited winery in the United States, are also self-guided and include complimentary tastings of Biltmore's award-winning wines.

In addition to the daytime visits guests can make reservations for special evening tours. Christmas Candlelight Evenings are a popular treat for those who want to experience the house filled with glowing candles and crackling fireplaces. Over 500 luminarias line the front lawn, beckoning guests to spend a warm holiday evening. During Christmas candlelight evenings, each of Biltmore's three restaurants offer holiday dinning.

*OPPOSITE: Pineapples and citrus fruits, considered delicacies, often appeared in arrangements on nineteenth-century Christmas tables*

## PUNCH FOR A BRUNCH

2  48-ounce cans pineapple juice

4  12-ounce cans frozen
orange juice concentrate

4  12-ounce cans frozen
lemonade concentrate

2  2-liter bottles of ginger ale

2  2-liter bottles club soda

*Mix* all ingredients in large punch bowl. Serve very cold. Makes 2½ gallons or 80 4-ounce servings.

—THE MAST INN, *Valle Crucis*

## CHRISTMAS MORNING CASSEROLE

1 pound hot sausage

6 slices white bread

¼ pound sharp cheddar, grated

8 large eggs, beaten

2 cups whole milk

1 teaspoon salt

1 teaspoon pepper

dash Worcestershire sauce

dash hot pepper sauce

*Preheat* oven to 300° F.

*Fry* sausage until done but not brown, drain. Crumble up bread and add to sausage. Place in casserole and sprinkle with cheese.

*Beat* together eggs, milk, salt, pepper and sauces. Pour over casserole. Cover and let stand overnight in refrigerator.

*Bake* uncovered for 50 minutes. Slice and serve.

*Serves* 10-12

—NAOMI WILLIS, *Asheville*

## HOT CINNAMON FRUIT

½ cup cinnamon candies

1 cup orange juice

2 tablespoons butter

2 tablespoons brown sugar

1 can apricot halves

1 can pear halves

1 can peach halves

1 can pineapple chunks

1 small jar maraschino cherries

*Preheat* oven to 300° F.

*Melt* cinnamon candies, together with orange juice, over low heat. Add butter and brown sugar. Cook until butter is melted and sugar is dissolved.

*Drain* juices from apricots, pears, peaches, pineapples and maraschino cherries.

*Add* juices to the candy mixture and cook until slightly thickened. Place fruit in casserole. Pour juices over fruit and bake for 20 minutes.

—NAOMI WILLIS, *Asheville*

*The Groaning Board, said to groan with the weight of Christmas delights, Iredell House, Edenton*

# BISCOTTI

*Adapted from the Biscotti Di Prato recipe in* ITALY IN SMALL BITES *by Carol Field.*

2½ cups self-rising flour

1 cup sugar

3 eggs

1 teaspoon vanilla

1 cup pistachio nuts

½ cup chopped almonds

egg wash, made by beating together
    1 large egg and 1 teaspoon water

*Preheat* oven to 325° F.

*In the bowl* of an electric mixer fitted with a paddle attachment, blend the flour and sugar until well combined.

*In a small bowl,* whisk together the eggs and vanilla. Add to the flour mixture, beating until a dough is formed. Stir in the pistachios and almonds.

*Turn the dough* out onto a lightly floured surface, knead it several times, and divide it into fourths. With floured hands, form each piece of dough into a flattish log 11 inches long and 2 inches wide. Arrange the logs at least 3 inches apart on 2 large, buttered and floured baking sheets, and brush the the logs with the egg wash.

*Bake* for 30 minutes, then let them cool on the baking sheets on racks for 10 minutes.

*On a cutting board,* cut the logs on the diagonal into ¾-inch-thick slices. Arrange the biscotti, cut side down, on baking sheets, and bake them in a 325° oven for 3 minutes on each side, or until they are a pale gold.

*Transfer* the biscotti to racks to cool. Store in airtight containers.

*Makes* about 56 biscotti.

—**SUSAN GUEST,** *Hickory*

*No matter what time we got up on Christmas morning, it was always to the smell of baking ham —for our Christmas breakfast of country ham, grits, and red-eye gravy. And we always had chocolate covered peanuts. Once we got into them, they didn't last long.*

—**BILL PITTMAN,** *Wilson*

*It wouldn't be Christmas without pecan sticky buns for breakfast.*

—**BETH WORKMAN,** *Raleigh*

## DRIED APPLE STACK CAKE

*Cake*

| | |
|---|---|
| 2⅔ cups plain flour | ½ cup butter or margarine |
| 1 teaspoon soda | 2 eggs |
| 1 teaspoon baking powder | |
| 1 teaspoon ground ginger | *Filling* |
| 1 teaspoon salt | 1 pound dried apples |
| ⅓ cup molasses | 1 cup brown sugar |
| 1 cup brown sugar | 1 cup white sugar |

*Preheat* oven to 325° F.

*Sift* together flour, soda, baking powder, salt and ginger.

*In a separate bowl,* mix molasses, brown sugar, butter and eggs. Stir dry ingredients into molasses mixture to form dough.

*Chill* in refrigerator 30 minutes. Divide dough into 6 equal parts. Place each piece of dough in the center of well-greased and floured pie pan, pressing to edges of pan. Fluted pie pans make the layers more attractive.

*Bake* for 15 minutes or until lightly brown. Do not bake more than 20 minutes.

*Cover* apples with water and cook until tender. Add sugar and mash until smooth. Spread hot cake layers with apple filling and stack.

—**DOLLY WHISNANT,** *Lenoir*

## BUTTERMILK PANCAKE MEDALLIONS

| | |
|---|---|
| 1 cup plain flour | ⅛ cup corn oil |
| 1 tablespoon baking powder | 1 large brown egg |
| 2 tablespoons sugar | ½ cup buttermilk |
| ½ teaspoon salt | water |
| ¼ teaspoon baking soda | butter |

*Mix* dry ingredients in food processor. Add oil, egg, buttermilk and pulse to blend. Add some water if needed to thin batter.

*Melt* 1 tablespoon butter in cast-iron skillet and wipe with paper towel. Spoon batter onto skillet in small medallions the size of silver dollars. Over a medium heat, cook until air bubbles appear, and then flip the medallions and cook to a golden brown. Keep medallions warm in pancake-keeper, or serve immediately with butter and maple syrup.

*Serves* 3 hungry people. You can double or triple the recipe as needed.

—**BETTY EIDENIER,** *Hillsborough*

# Chinqua-Penn Plantation

"Come, and you may find some mediation for the mind, some solace for the soul, some harmony for the heart…come!" This inviting Chinese saying is inscribed on one of the buildings at Chinqua-Penn Plantation. Named for the chinquapin, a dwarf chestnut tree, and for the original owners, Thomas Jefferson Penn and his wife, Betsey, Chinqua-Penn is one of the most unusual museums in the state.

Built in 1925, the 27-room manor house contains an eclectic collection of art and artifacts. Accumulated by the Penns during their international travels, this extensive collection of Oriental and religious art is one of the finest in North Carolina.

The grounds encompass 22 acres of manicured lawns and formal gardens, with greenhouses, pools, fountains, and a reproduction of a Chinese pagoda.

*The Breakfast Room, Chinqua-Penn, Reidsville*

During the month of December, Chinqua-Penn is open regularly for visitors. Wreaths and garlands made from hemlock, pine, and holly—all grown on the plantation—adorn the buildings. The manor house is filled with Christmas trees, poinsettias, and elaborate holiday arrangements.

Christmas music plays throughout the house, while outside the three-story clock tower chimes Christmas carols. In the evening, luminaries create a welcoming glow along the front drive and around the Versailles fountain.

*Winter sunrise,*
*Cape Hatteras*
*National Seashore*

*I like the custom that*
*some churches have of*
*singing Christmas hymns*
*for a Sunday or two after*
*Christmas day, and I wish*
*all churches would adopt*
*the practice. Christmas*
*programs and cantatas could*
*also be held during the week*
*following Christmas, not*
*in the hurried days before.*
*The birth of Christ was the*
*beginning not the end.*

**—JOHN HAWKINS**
*Lenoir*

*St. Matthew's Episcopal Church, near Todd*

*Our Christmas tradition begins with Advent and the making of a wreath and lighting the Advent candles. This is a time of quiet and peacefulness leading up to the excitement of Christmas. The children keep an Advent calendar. We keep a crèche in the living room, a manger scene we've created out of moss, dried flowers, honeycomb, and beeswax figurines. Each day Laurel moves Mary and Joseph closer toward the stable. The wise men follow and usually arrive at Epiphany.*

—**DAVID CROSBY,** *Hickory*

*OPPOSITE: Stained-glass window of Mary holding baby Jesus, St. Lawrence Catholic Church, Asheville*

"Mary, Great with Child," by Ben Long

On Christmas Eve the whole family gathers together at the home of Steve's parents. After a light meal, one person, usually his father, reads the Christmas story from the Bible to all of us gathered around. It brings back the real meaning of Christmas as we start our celebrations.

—**NANCY AND STEVE TRAMBLE**
*Granite Falls*

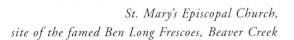

*St. Mary's Episcopal Church,*
*site of the famed Ben Long Frescoes, Beaver Creek*

# THE MOUNTAIN FRESCOES

Tucked into the northwest corner of North Carolina is a remote Episcopal parish, peopled with honest, but mostly poor mountain folks. Surprisingly, two tiny churches within this parish are the sites of some of North Carolina's greatest art treasures.

In 1973, parish priest Father Faulton Hodge met artist Ben Long, a Statesville native who had been studying fresco painting in Florence, Italy. Fresco painting, the art of painting directly on wet plaster, requires considerable talent and training. Long had worked on some of the great European frescoes, and he wished to do an original in a North Carolina church.

Turned away by larger city churches, the artist was welcomed by an enthusiastic but impoverished Father Hodge. Just one year earlier, when Father Hodge had arrived at the parish, he discovered that one of its churches had closed and the other was seriously declining. Things had improved, but there was no budget for art. Long offered to give his work to the church as a gift.

Long made the first sketches for the frescoes in a Blowing Rock garage. He used an unidentified Boone girl as the model for Mary's face, and his pregnant wife, Diane, posed for the rest of the painting. The beautiful finished piece, entitled "Mary, Great with Child," hangs in Saint Mary's Episcopal Church in Beaver Creek.

With the help of a group of volunteers, Long created four other frescos. They appear in Saint Mary's and in Holy Trinity Church in Glendale Springs. Numerous parishioners were immortalized as characters in the frescoes, including Father Hodge, who appears as a servant.

In the days of Father Hodge, children wove greenery into Christmas wreaths, then scattered throughout the hills to carol and deliver the wreaths and baskets of food to the poor. Nowadays the highlight of the season is the Christmas Eve service: As the Christmas story is read, children assemble a small crèche in front of the altar. The crèche remains there throughout the holidays.

People of many faiths and nationalities come to Ashe and Allegheny Counties just to see the internationally acclaimed frescoes by Ben Long.

*Our family always attends
the Mount Carmel Church
on Christmas Eve to see the
annual Christmas program.*

**—LIVONIA SHACKELFORD**
*Nann's Harbor*

*"His heart was filled. His
happiness was bigger than the
Christmas laurel. It filled the
little Church house, maybe it
even filled the whole world."*

**—GLORIA HOUSTON**
*printed with permission by
Philomel Books Littlejim's Gift:
An Appalachian Christmas Story*

*Christmas Eve sunset service in the historic Chapel of Rest, Patterson*

### *Christmas Prayer*
*from Pine Crest Inn, Tryon*

*We are gathered today
To celebrate the birth of our Lord.
Let us praise him at all times;
Especially in this season
When we are joined together
with those we love.
Let us give thanks.*

*AMEN*

*Lighting the Advent candle,
Christmas Eve at Northminister
Presbyterian Church, Hickory*

*We go as a family to candlelight
service Christmas Eve and then open
packages Christmas morn, followed
by Christmas brunch.*

**—KAY B. WEAVER,** *Hickory*

# THE POEM THAT NEVER WENT AWAY

In the final years of the Great Depression and during the war years that followed, Christmas Eve with the family of Douglas and Cecil Rights was story time. Douglas, pastor of the Trinity Moravian Church in Winston-Salem, sat in a wicker rocking chair telling stories and reading verses beside an open fire, one child on his lap and three others gathered around the hearth.

Years after his parents' deaths, one of the sons, also an ordained Moravian minister, was preparing a Christmas Eve message for his own congregation when he remembered a poem that had been a regular part of his family's Christmas tradition around the fire. It was a poem about keeping Christmas alive throughout the year. Desiring to share the poem with his congregation, he went to the Christmas books that had belonged to his father. It was not there. He searched the city library, but without success.

For ten Advent seasons he looked for the lost poem, until one day, while rummaging through a dusty box of his father's papers, he uncovered "Christmas Came to Our House and Never Went Away." The surprising discovery revealed the name Douglas L. Rights typed at the bottom of the yellowed page. The poem had been written by his father.

**—BURTON J. RIGHTS,** *Clemmons*

We especially love it when all our kids are home. The grandchildren light the Advent candles and they sing "Happy Birthday" to Jesus.

**—MARY AND GEORGE PARKERSON**
*Durham*

## Christmas Came to Our House and Never Went Away

*Used to think that Christmas was nothing but a day*
*To get a lot of presents and to give a lot away.*
*Shouted, "Merry Christmas," and helped to trim the tree—*
*Just a day of Christmas was all that I could see.*
*But I found that Christmas is more than any day*
*Since Christmas came to our house and never went away.*

*Struck me of a sudden that friendliness and cheer*
*Were meant to be on duty more than one day in a year.*
*If you're happy Christmas, why not the day before*
*And the day that follows, and so on evermore?*
*Got to thinkin' of it an' that is why I say,*
*Christmas came to our house and never went away.*

*Lots of us go plodding along the road of life*
*An' think one day of gladness will make up for all strife.*
*But the Christmas spirit can show you how you need*
*To make each day a Christmas in thought and word and deed.*
*Used to pack the kindness in camphor balls next day,*
*Till Christmas came to our house and never went away.*

**—DOUGLAS L. RIGHTS** *(1891-1956)*

St. Mary's Episcopal Church, Blowing Rock

## A Ballad of Christmas
### BY ELIZABETH UTTERBACK

A great star glowed rightly down over the pasture,
The angels sung hymn—tunes in a rare godly band,
As Mary birthed Jesus in a little ole cow-shed,
An' the glory of Christmas come down on the land!

The little lambs seen it an' kneeled in their wonder,
The cows chewed an' gazed with a marveling eye,
An' Mary wrapped Jesus in an old piece of kivver,
An' rocked him to sleep with the creatures close by.

She sung as she rocked him, for she never knowed then,
The days when her son would be nailed on a tree,
She jest knowed the light ringed his head on her bosom,
As pretty a sight as you ever could see.

It happened out yonder—t' other side of the mountain…
In some furrin' part, I don't jest understand,
That Mary birthed Jesus in a little ole cow-shed,
An' the glory of Christmas come down on the land!

Reprinted with permission

I just love the poem "A Ballad of Christmas" by
Elizabeth Utterback. It has become part of my
Christmas tradition—particularly the last verse.

**—BETTY TILLEY**, Montreat

*The living Christmas pageant at Antioch Baptist Church*

Every Christmas Eve in our little church, we had
the Christmas Pageant. Sheets were strung across
the front of the church for a backdrop. There were
candles in the window and a big tree in the front.
Because the only heat came from a big pot-bellied
stove, we all tried to sit as close to it as possible.
Afterwards Santa always came bearing small gifts
like oranges, which were difficult to get in those days.

—**JANE PRUDEN,** Asheville

*Antioch Baptist Church near Taylorsville and Bethlehem*

# Old Salem

In the mid-1700s Moravian settlers arrived in North Carolina, establishing the towns of Bethabara and Salem. As was the Moravian tradition, they celebrated their religion with love feasts and musical services. Today in Old Salem, many modern-day Moravians still celebrate the holidays as they have for more than 200 years.

Moravians keep Christmas simple. There is always music, candlelight concerts, love feasts, and voices raised in praise of the season. Decorations include greenery, nativity scenes, Moravian stars, and illuminations. One of the loveliest historical decorations, illuminations are pieces of translucent paper with pictures and designs drawn on them. Lighted from behind by candles they create an almost magical luminescence.

## THE MORAVIAN LOVE FEAST

The first Moravian love feast was celebrated Germany in 1727, and this simple ceremony continues to this day as an expression of Christian unity and good will. People of all denominations are invited to love feasts, which can be held throughout the year, but are particularly beautiful on Christmas Eve.

*Serving sweet buns at a Moravian love feast, New Hope Moravian Church, Newton*

Primarily a song service, the Christmas love feast begins with prayer, a devotional address, and the reading of the Christmas story. During the service, as the choir sings, women of the church, dressed in white dresses and caps, serve sweetened buns in wicker baskets to the congregation. The men of the church pass out mugs of coffee, pre-sweetened with sugar and cream.

*The highlight of the Christmas season for us was going to the candlelight love feast on Christmas Eve at Ardmore Moravian Church. Nothing shines as brightly in my mind's eye as the picture of the red-trimmed beeswax candles held high above the heads of my children at the close of the service, and there is no sweeter sound than that of their small voices singing "Morning Star."*

*—MARY A. ALSPAUGH*
*Winston-Salem*

Once all have been served, the feast is blessed and the minister and congregation eat and drink together. At the close of the service, candles are lighted by each member of the congregation, illuminating the darkened church.

## CANDLES

Candles play a significant part in the Moravian celebrations. Early records tell of candles with red bands being given to children at the Christmas Eve love feast. Moravian women in Old Salem still hand-dip beeswax candles to be used in love feasts. During the holiday season at historic Bethabara Park, candlelight tours welcome visitors to the restored Gemeinhaus, built in 1788 by the early settlers.

*Moravian women still hand-dip candles to use in love feast services*

## CHRISTMAS PYRAMIDS

Candles, Bible verses, straw stars, sweets, and fruits are typically hung on Moravian Christmas pyramids, a tradition brought to North Carolina from Germany via Pennsylvania. Two to three feet tall, these beautiful decorations resemble trees but are actually four poles attached at the top to form a pyramid. The poles are then wrapped with greenery and decorated. As with most Moravian practices, many of the items hung on the pyramid have religious significance. A small Nativity scene is often placed at its base.

## THE CANDLE TEA

Dating from 1929, the candle tea is a more modern tradition, although it is held in the historic Single Brothers' House, which was built in 1769 to house the unmarried men of the community. Costumed hostesses greet the guests and guide them through the house, where they attend a hymn-sing in the chapel, observe the art of candle making,

*One of my favorite decorations is a large Moravian star on our front porch. It is a star that was used in downtown Winston-Salem for seventeen years, from 1957 to 1984.*

**— CAROL QUINN,** *Advance*

and enjoy sugar cake and coffee. The final stop is in the cellar, where the Christmas *putz* is displayed. Putz means "to decorate" and is usually applied to elaborate Nativity scenes. In the Single Brothers' House there are two putz displays: one of the town of Salem during the 1800s and the other of Bethlehem and surrounding countryside as it would have looked on the night of Christ's birth.

Christmas in Old Salem highlights hundreds of years of tradition and deep religious conviction. It is filled with music and light, history and faith, unity and goodwill—a very special Christmas experience.

*Throughout North Carolina, but especially in the Winston-Salem area, people decorate with the sixteen-point Moravian star*

*Lighting the Menorah*

# Hanukkah—Festival of Lights

On the evening of the 25th day of Kislev, in the Hebrew lunar calendar, the North Carolina Jewish community begins one of the most joyous celebrations of the Jewish year—Hanukkah. Also known as the Festival of Lights, Hanukkah lasts eight days, each one celebrated by the lighting of a candle in the Menorah, adding a new candle each night. The nine candles of the Menorah (one to light the other eight) signify a miraculous event in Hebrew history.

In 165 B.C. Judah Maccabee, his brothers, and a small Hebrew army defeated the Syrian tyrant Antiochus. With great joy the people cleansed their temple of the hated idols left behind by the Syrians. All they could find was one small cruse of consecrated oil to re-dedicate the temple to God. It was not nearly enough. In faith, they lit the oil anyway, and to their great amazement, it burned for eight days until new oil could be made.

Because Hanukkah is based on the lunar calendar, the dates of this festival vary each year, the earliest can be November 28 and the latest December 24. Celebrations throughout the state are filled with music and high spirits. There is a great deal of visiting, a time when children spin the dreidel, a simple four-sided top on which appear the Hebrew words "A great miracle happened there," which figure in the scoring of the game. At home, children light a Menorah and receive one small gift each night.

# Native American Festival of Nature

Evidence of human existence in North Carolina dates back approximately 10,000 years, and over the years, peoples of many names have lived here. Today more than 80,000 Native Americans make North Carolina home. The major tribes include the Cherokee, Coharie, Haliwa-Saponi, Lumbee, Meherrin, and Waccamaw-Siouan. Many other tribes have smaller representations throughout the state.

Native Americans celebrate the coming of winter by honoring the fall harvest, a time to thank the Great Spirit for bringing food enough for another year. During the month of November, Native American heritage is officially observed in North Carolina with gatherings, dances, music, and food.

Numerous Native American associations have sprung up in North Carolina to preserve the native culture and pass on traditional ways to the next generation. Observing the harvest is celebration for young and old alike. In addition to these observances, many Native Americans have adopted Christianity and celebrate the holiday within their own denominations, which they find compatible with their close ties to the earth.

*Indian women spend months hand-sewing and beading the elaborate regalia they wear when dancing in North Carolina's Native American Cultural Center events, such as this one in Charlotte*

# Kwanzaa Festival of Unity

First established in 1965 in Los Angeles after the unrest in Watts, the African-American celebration of Kwanzaa is observed by people of African descent all over the country, including North Carolinian's. Kwanzaa means "first" in Swahili and it encompasses the seven days from December 26 through January 1. The days are filled with music, dancing, art, crafts, storytelling, prayer, feasting, and candle lighting. Central to the symbolism of Kwanzaa is the *kinara*, a candle holder with red, green, and black candles. Each candle signifies one of the seven basic principles of the harvest in Africa. One principle is emphasized each day.

## PRINCIPLES OF KWANZAA

1. UMOJA (Unity)

2. KUJICHAGULIA (Self-determination)

3. UJIMA (Collective Work and Responsibility)

4. UJAMMA (Cooperative Economics)

5. NIA (Purpose)

6. KUUMBA (Creativity)

7. IMANI (Faith)

*Seven candles of the* kinara *represent the seven principles of Kwanzaa*

*OPPOSITE: Moses Cone Estate, Blowing Rock*

*Shrimp boat, Oyster Creek, Carteret County*

# Morning Star

1. Morn-ing Star, O cheer-ing sight! Ere thou cam'st, how dark earth's
2. Morn-ing Star, thy glor-ry bright far ex-cels the sun's clear
3. Thy glad beams, thou Morn-ing Star, cheer the na-tions near and
4. Morn-ing Star, my soul's true light, tar-ry not, dis-pel my

night! Morn-ing Star, O cheer-ing sight! Ere thou
light. Morn-ing Star, thy glo-ry bright far ex-
far. Thy glad beams, thou Morn-ing Star, cheer the
night. Morn-ing Star, my soul's true light, tar-ry

cam'st, how dark earth's night! Je-sus mine, in me shine; in me
cels the sun's clear light. Je-sus be, con-stant-ly, con-stant-
na-tions near and far. Thee we own, Lord a-lone, Lord a-
not, dis-pel my night. Je-sus mine, in me shine; in me

shine, Je-sus mine; fill my heart with light di-vine.
ly, Je-sus be more than thou-sand suns to me.
lone, thee we own, our dear Sav-ior, God's dear Son.
shine, Je-sus mine; fill my heart with light di-vine.

From *Moravian Book of Worship*, 1995. Reprinted with permission.

*Massive stone fireplaces anchor each end of the Grove Park Inn's Great Hall*

# Christmas at the Grove Park Inn

When the spectacular Grove Park Inn in Asheville opened in 1913, it was hailed by high society as the finest resort in existence. A walk through the hotel's great halls gives one the feeling of being surrounded by history, as the corridors are lined with rows upon rows of photographs of famous people who have stayed at the inn. Wilson, Taft, Hoover, and Roosevelt—the Grove Park Inn has been the choice of presidents. Writer F. Scott Fitzgerald lived in the hotel for a time. Other former guests include Thomas Edison, John J. Pershing, Will Rogers, Walter Cronkite, and Michael Jordan, to name just a few.

At Christmastime, the biggest celebrity at the Grove Park Inn is a teddy bear. Known as Major Bear, this larger-than-life-size live puppet is the Grove Park Inn's holiday ambassador. The original "teddy" bear was given to Eleanor Roosevelt by her uncle, Teddy Roosevelt, when she was just a child. Legend has it that when the Roosevelt children stayed at the inn, the bear was accidentally left behind.

*Grove Park Inn, Asheville*

The Grove Park Inn has become one of the most loved and visited Christmas attractions in western North Carolina. From its giant stone fireplaces to its uniquely decorated Christmas trees, the Grove Park Inn is transformed into a veritable wonderland during the holiday season.

Arriving through the massive oak doors, visitors are treated to a spectacularly decorated twenty-foot-tall Fraser fir, standing center stage in the eighty-by-forty-foot Great Hall. Throughout the inn are fifty-seven living trees, each one distinctly decorated. The inn's grounds crew and floral shop use more than 12,700 ornaments, 11,000 lights, 1,000 poinsettia plants as well as an assortment of other holiday decorations, including 200 antique and reproduction toys.

The truly special Christmas event at the Grove Park Inn is the annual gingerbread house contest. The inn's pastry chef provides a free workshop on building houses of gingerbread, candies, and other edibles. Dozens of confectionary creations are entered each year, and the winning houses are displayed in a village-like setting, complete with antique electric trains—much to the delight of little children.

Throughout the holiday season, chefs prepare buffets and dinners for hundreds of parties as well as the inn's renowned restaurants. And through it all, Major Bear warmly welcomes everyone.

*One of numerous entries in the Grove Park Inn's annual gingerbread house contest*

*Wassail Rosé, Pasteis and
Governor Hunt's Favorite
Holiday Cookies*

# WASSAIL ROSÉ

2 quarts apple cider

1½ quarts cranberry juice

3 to 4 tablespoons
 orange juice concentrate

½ cup brown sugar

whole cloves

1 orange

1 lemon

2 to 3 cinnamon sticks

2 quarts good quality rosé wine

*Mix* cider, cranberry juice, orange juice concentrate and brown sugar together in pot. Heat to boiling, then reduce heat and simmer about 20 minutes.

*Stick* cloves in the orange and lemon and cut into about 5 slices each. It is easiest to arrange cloves in rings around each fruit, leaving enough space to slice between rings. Add slices to simmering pot along with cinnamon sticks, and simmer 10 more minutes.

*Add* wine and heat—*but do not boil.*

*Carefully* transfer orange and lemon slices to punch bowl. Pour 2 to 4 cups of hot wassail into the bowl and allow it to sit long enough to warm the bowl so there is no danger of it breaking. Slowly add remaining wassail. Serve in punch cups. Makes 45 4-ounce servings

—**THE MAST INN,** *Vallee Crucis*

*Every Christmas Eve we invite family and friends over to our house for an open house. We fix brown sugar meatballs, chicken pie, broccoli bacon salad, Mexican corn bread, pumpkin pie, and Toll House cookies. We listen to Johnny Mathis, and each child gets to open one present.*

—**KNIGHT CHAMBERLAIN**
*Lumberton*

# PASTEIS

*From Brazil, pasteis are heavenly little fried pies filled with a meat or cheese mixture and sold on almost every street corner.*

*Dough*

2 cups all-purpose flour

½ cup warm water

½ teaspoon salt

3 tablespoons cooking oil

2 teaspoons white wine

*Cheese Filling*

8 ounces ricotta cheese

2 eggs

¾ cup Parmesan cheese

salt and pepper

paprika

*Measure* flour into bowl and add remaining dough ingredients. Mix lightly with a fork, then with fingers to make a smooth pastry. Set aside.

*Mix* ricotta, eggs and Parmesan cheese until well blended. Add salt and pepper and paprika to taste.

*Pinch* off bits of dough and roll out on floured surface into small circles—about 3 inches in diameter. Place a teaspoon of cheese mixture in center, fold over and press edges with a fork to seal.

*Fry* in deep fat until golden brown, sprinkle with extra Parmesan cheese, drain on paper towels and serve immediately. Makes about 20.

Pasteis may be made a day or two in advance. Stack in layers with waxed paper between each layer. Cover tightly and refrigerate. Use leftover cheese filling in lasagna or, for a quick snack, spread it on bread and broil until it begins to brown.

—**THE MAST INN,** *Valle Crucis*

# CREAM OF CHRISTMAS SOUP

1 medium onion, chopped

2 tablespoons butter

4 packages chopped broccoli,
   cooked and drained

2 14½-ounce cans chicken broth

2 cans cream of potato soup

2 cans cream of mushroom soup

1 7-ounce jar of pimentos, drained

3 soup cans milk

1 teaspoon salt

½ teaspoon pepper

1 tablespoon white wine

Worchestershire sauce

4 drops hot sauce

*Sauté* onion in butter. Add other ingredients and simmer.

—CAROL QUINN, *Advance*

I have been collecting Spode Christmas tree china for over 25 years, and I love to use the tureen for my Cream of Christmas Soup.

—CAROL QUINN, *Advance*

# WINTER SQUASH CASSEROLE

3 cups cooked and mashed winter squash

½ to ¾ cup sugar

½ teaspoon salt

2 eggs

⅓ stick butter

½ cup sweet milk

2 teaspoons vanilla

*Topping*

⅓ cup melted butter

1 cup brown sugar

1 cup chopped nuts

⅓ cup flour

*Preheat* oven to 350° F.

*Mix* first seven ingredients and place in a casserole dish. Mix topping ingredients and spread over squash. Bake for 30 minutes.

—MARY ELDER, *Banner Elk*

On Christmas Eve we always had Brunswick stew and grandmother's corn bread. Then we'd go next door to David's and drink and put toys together.

—JIM HATHAWAY
*Elizabeth City*

# CORN CASSEROLE

2 cans shoe peg (white) corn, drained

1 small square cream cheese

¼ stick butter or margarine

1 small can El Paso mild
   green chili peppers, chopped and drained

1 to 3 tablespoons chopped pimentos

*Heat* first three ingredients and stir until butter and cheese melt. Stir in peppers and pimentos. Serve warm or at room temperature.

—JANE ROBINSON, *Boone*

# GIGI'S CORNBREAD

1 cup flour

1 cup cornmeal (not self-rising)

½ teaspoon salt

¼ teaspoon baking soda

3 tablespoons baking powder

1 tablespoon sugar

3 to 4 tablespoons margarine, melted

1 egg

2 cups buttermilk

*Preheat* oven to 400° F.

*Beat* all ingredients together. Put into a greased, 9-inch pie plate.

*Bake* for ½ hour.

—DONA DYCHE, *Boone*

# CHRISTMAS CRANBERRY SALAD

3 to 4 cups cranberries

1 cup water or orange juice

2 packages orange Jell-O

¼ cup pecan pieces

baking spray for mold

*Bring* cranberries just barely to a boil in a small amount of water (do not cook them). Combine cranberries, water or juice, and gelatin in a food processor and grind until cranberries are chopped and mixture foams. Add pecan pieces.

*Pour* salad into individual molds lightly coated with baking spray, or into one large mold. You can also pour it into flat baking pan and use cookie cutter to cut out shapes. Children *love* this!

—GLORIA HOUSTON

On Christmas Eve we generally have a simple supper, perhaps chili, before attending worship services. Our family opens gifts on Christmas morning. For dinner it's always ham and turkey with oyster dressing.

—COL. DWIGHT JARVIS
*Emerald Isle*

# TOMATO ASPIC WITH CREAM CHEESE FILLING

2 cups tomato juice or V-8 juice

½ bay leaf

½ teaspoon salt

1 stalk of celery, chopped

dash of cayenne or black pepper

1 envelope unflavored Knox gelatin

¼ cup cold water

1 tablespoon mild apple vinegar

1 tablespoon finely grated onion zest

*Filling*

½ envelope Knox gelatin

2 tablespoons cold water

1 4-ounce package cream cheese, softened

½ cup mayonnaise

2 drops Tabasco sauce

⅛ teaspoon finely grated onion zest

½ teaspoon salt

*Mix* tomato juice, bay leaf, salt, celery, and cayenne pepper. Boil 10 minutes or slightly longer to blend the spices. Meanwhile soften gelatin in cold water. Add gelatin to the hot tomato mixture and stir until dissolved. Add the vinegar and onion. Strain the mixture to remove the celery pieces and discard them. Then pour half of the aspic mixture into a salad mold that has been rinsed with cold water. Place this into the refrigerator to gel. Keep the other half of the aspic at room temperature.

*To make filling* combine in gelatin and cold water in the top of a double boiler and stir over boiling water until dissolved. Add cream cheese, mayonnaise, and seasonings to the gelatin.

*When portion* in the refrigerator is almost jelled, spoon the cheese mixture on top and refrigerate until this has almost jelled. Then spoon on the remaining aspic layer and refrigerate until completely jelled.

*To remove* the aspic from the mold, set the bottom of the mold into warm water for a few seconds before turning out onto the platter. Cut the aspic into thin slices and serve over lettuce leaves.

You can make this in any shaped container, but a bundt cake pan makes a very pretty table decoration.

—ELLEN P. HARDY, *Fayetteville*

*We sit around in our pajamas all day and do nothing but eat and drink.*

—J. LANGSTON
*Banner Elk*

*The Grove Park' Inn's Christmas Feast: Traditional Turkey with Sausage Stuffing, Butternut Squash and Brie Soup, and Christmas Stollen*

# TRADITIONAL TURKEY WITH SAUSAGE STUFFING

20 pound turkey

1 pound chopped turkey sausage or
 ground turkey meat

½ cup butter or margarine

1 large onion, chopped

1 cup chopped celery

2½ cups turkey or chicken broth

1 loaf white or whole wheat bread, diced

4 cups crumbled corn bread or
 1 package corn bread stuffing mix

1 tablespoon thyme

1 tablespoon sage

*Preheat* oven to 350° F.

*Cook* turkey sausage in 10-inch skillet over medium heat until browned, breaking apart with fork. Stir in ½ cup butter, onion and celery. Cook until celery is tender, about 5 minutes. Stir occasionally. Add broth and bring to a boil. Remove from heat.

*In large bowl,* combine meat mixture with white bread (or whole wheat), corn bread, thyme and sage. Stir until well mixed. Salt to taste. Stuff turkey and cook in separate roasting pan for approximately 2½ to 3 hours, or to an internal temperature of 165° F. Serves 20.

—**FRED DAWI,** *Banquet Chef*
*Grove Park Inn, Asheville*

# HOLIDAY OYSTER DRESSING

1 16-ounce loaf white bread, toasted

¼ pound saltine crackers

3 eggs, beaten

½ pint oysters, chopped

salt and pepper

4 teaspoons baking powder

1 cup chopped celery

1 teaspoon sage

2 cups cooked chicken or turkey meat

½ gallon broth
 (enough to make real sloppy)

*Preheat* oven to 350° F.

*Crush* toasted bread and crackers and put in a mixing bowl. Add all remaining ingredients and mix well.

*Bake* 1 hour in greased and floured pan.

—**ARDELIA V. WOMBLE,** *Winston-Salem*

# CORNBREAD DRESSING

2 packages Jiffy cornbread mix

1 cup chopped celery

½ cup finely chopped onion
 (or more, to taste)

½ cup butter or margarine

1½ teaspoons salt

1 teaspoon pepper

1 teaspoon sage to taste

2 eggs

1 can turkey or chicken broth

*Preheat* oven to 400° F.

*Sauté* celery and onion in butter till tender. Add to bread mix. Add salt, pepper and sage. Add eggs and enough broth to make a moist mixture.

*Spread* mixture in 9 x 13-inch pan. Bake for 30 to 45 minutes until browned. Serves 12.

—**JOYCE S. CLAYTON,** *Hickory*

*I am a native of Highlands and have lived here all my life. I'm lucky that my husband's family and my own live here too. We get together at my husband's parents on Christmas Eve for finger sandwiches and snick-snacks. Christmas morning we have a huge breakfast cooked by my mother-in-law, then it's back home to get everything ready for my family. My relatives arrive around 2:00 P.M., and we have turkey and dressing, gravy, ham, homemade rolls, mashed potatoes, sweet potatoes, green beans, creamed corn, and usually something new that someone decides to try.*

—**GLENDA DILLS,** *Highlands*

*In addition to traditional turkey and all the trimmings, we like mincemeat pie and especially the Georgia biscuits I learned to make from my mother.*

—**MARY PARKERSON**
*Durham*

# CHRISTMAS STOLLEN

1 package dry yeast

1 cup lukewarm milk

3 cups bread flour

¼ cup butter, softened

1 egg yolk

1 tablespoon sugar

1 teaspoon salt

1 teaspoon ground cinnamon

¼ teaspoon allspice

1 cup mixed candied fruit, soaked in rum

almond paste

1 egg white

*Preheat* oven to 350° F.

*Mix* yeast with milk. Add remaining ingredients except almond paste and egg white. Knead by hand for 5 minutes. Let double in size for one hour.

*Roll* dough out into a circle. Mix almond paste with egg white, and place almond mixture on one side of the dough. Roll up and let rest for one hour.

*Bake* for 30 to 35 minutes. Brush melted butter over bread. Roll in powdered and granulated sugar mixture.

—**ETHAN WHITENER,** *Executive Sous Chef, Grove Park Inn Resort, Asheville.*

*When our daughters were quite young we began a tradition of having one special gift for each to open on Christmas Eve. Then we go to a candlelight church service, and after that walk through the Grove Park Inn, enjoying their decorations.*

—**JOY MINTON,** *Asheville*

*Native North Carolinian Ethan Whitener, the Grove Park Inn's executive sous chef*

# BUTTERNUT SQUASH & BRIE SOUP

2 butternut squash, peeled and diced

1 large onion, diced

1 gallon chicken stock

½ teaspoon white pepper

1 pound Brie cheese, cut into small cubes

½ gallon milk

*Combine* squash, onion, chicken stock and white pepper and allow to cook until squash is soft and stock is reduced by half. Add brie cheese and milk. Simmer for 15 to 20 minutes, stirring frequently to reduce the chance of lumping. Garnish with slices of red, yellow and green peppers and serve immediately.

—**ETHAN WHITENER,** *Executive Sous Chef, Grove Park Inn, Asheville*

# PAN-SEARED DUCK BREAST WITH LINGONBERRY SAUCE

4 boneless duck breasts, skin removed

1 tablespoon olive oil

pinch salt and pepper

*Marinade*

1 cup olive oil

½ cup white wine

3 sprigs fresh thyme

2 sprigs fresh rosemary

pinch salt and cracked black pepper

*Sauce*

3 cups reduced veal stock

1 cup red wine

1 cup lingonberries

1 tablespoon chopped shallots

1 teaspoon lemon juice

1 tablespoon unsalted butter

salt and pepper to taste

**Combine** marinade ingredients and marinate duck breasts for at least two hours.

**Season** duck with salt and pepper and sear both sides in olive oil. Place in 375° F. oven for 8 to 10 minutes until medium rare. Remove from pan and keep in warm space.

**Remove** excess oil, add shallots, and sauté until translucent. Deglaze with red wine and simmer until reduced by half. Add veal stock and lingonberries, reduce by half again. Then add butter, lemon juice, salt and pepper, and stir until butter is melted.

**Return duck** to oven for 3 minutes. Remove and slice into equal portions, sliced across the grain for best results.

**Fan** each duck breast on a plate and ladle with 2-ounces of sauce over each portion.

—**FEARRINGTON HOUSE**, *Pittsboro*

*My favorite Christmas recipe is a beautiful red and white salad that really hits the spot with so many heavy holiday foods. It is a recipe my eighty-year-old mother has always made for our family Christmas dinner.*

—**ELLEN P. HARDY**, *Fayetteville*

*We eat Christmas dinner at noon on Christmas Eve, after toasting with glogg. Homemade sausage is a favorite as well as many other Swedish Christmas foods. We are first generation Americans and still make the traditional dishes.*

—**LENA BENGTSON**, *Conover*

*Christmas at the House in the Horseshoe, Carthage*

## SHRIMP NOEL CASSEROLE

¾ to 1 pound fresh mushrooms

¼ cup butter or margarine

2 to 3 cups cleaned and cooked
    shrimp (or 1 to 2 cups crab meat)

2 to 3 cups cooked rice

½ to 1 cup chopped green pepper

½ to 1 cup chopped onion

½ cup chopped celery

¼ cup chopped pimento (2-ounce jar)

1  28-ounce can tomatoes, drained and
    cut into ½- to 1-inch pieces

¼ to ¾ teaspoon salt to taste

½ to 1 teaspoon chili powder to taste

½ cup butter or margarine, melted

*Preheat* oven to 300° F.

*Cook* the mushrooms in the ¼ cup of butter just till tender. Combine with shrimp (or crab), rice, vegetables, and seasonings. Place in a greased 2-quart casserole; don't fill higher than ½ inch from top. Pour ½ cup of melted butter over casserole.

*Bake* for 50 to 60 minutes. Then trim with a wreath of parsley and stuffed olive slices.

*The uncooked casserole* can be frozen and cooked at later date. The 2-quart casserole makes 6-8 servings. If you use the larger amounts of rice and vegetables, you may have enough leftover for another 1- to 1½-quart casserole.

—**COL. CARLTON C. COOK,** *High Point*

The highlight of our Afro-American family holiday is the Christmas Eve program, when several families gather around the Christmas tree. A mistress of ceremonies is selected, and she oversees the evening's program, which traditionally involves welcoming, remembering, and rejoicing.

The program includes singing Christmas carols, reading the story of the Christ child, reciting favorite Bible verses, and, at the conclusion, a group sing-along of "The Twelve Days of Christmas" with different family members singing each verse and everyone joining in for the chorus.

The festivities generate much camaraderie among both young and old. And because we are all amateurs, some of the performances are very humorous.

During the program we feast on eggnog and fruitcake, along with favorite family recipes. We try to make the evening educational, creative, and inspirational—in the spirit of Christmas.

—**LILLIE CUTHRELL**
*Winston-Salem*

## AFRICAN CHICKEN AND GREENS

3- to 4-pound chicken, cut up

1 large onion, chopped

1 large carrot, peeled and sliced

3 tablespoons butter

salt

1 clove garlic, minced

2 teaspoons ground coriander

3 10-ounce packages frozen spinach
    or collard greens, thawed

*Put* chicken pieces in large pot with onions and carrots. Cover with water and simmer for one hour. Remove chicken. Save onion and carrots. Discard stock.

*Melt* butter in large fry pan. Add salt, garlic and coriander. Brown chicken on all sides. Remove from pan. Place thawed greens in fry pan, and top with layer of browned chicken. Cover and simmer for 15 to 25 minutes. Serve with rice.

*Popular in Africa, this recipe will be an authentic addition to Kwanzaa celebrations.*

—**LILLIE CUTHRELL,** *Winston-Salem*

*North Carolina's Executive Mansion, Raleigh*

# Christmas at the Executive Mansion

For more than a hundred years, North Carolina governors and their families have resided in the Executive Mansion. Designed by noted architects Samuel Sloan and A. G. Bauer, the mansion is one of the finest examples of Queen Anne Victorian architecture in the state.

With its sixteen-foot ceilings, gracious rooms, and massive grand staircase, the Executive Mansion is ideally suited for holiday entertaining. Guests are greeted with magnificent holiday decorations as they proceed from the grand hallway into the dining room, the library, and the ladies' and gentlemen's parlors. The old-fashioned aroma of spiced cider adds to the Christmas atmosphere.

The official state Christmas tree in the gentlemen's parlor, is a Fraser fir decorated with items associated with North Carolina, such as dogwood blossoms, cardinals, Scotch bonnets, pine cones, and sand dollars. On mantles and tables are arrangements made from plants indigenous to

*Draperies made of white pine and Fraser fir adorn the library*

**Executive Mansion**
**Raleigh, North Carolina**

# HOT SPICED CIDER

1 gallon cider
juice of 2 lemons
6 cinnamon sticks

5 whole cloves
pinch of nutmeg
½ cup brown sugar

*Heat* above ingredients until sugar is dissolved. Set aside for ½ hour and serve.

—MRS. CAROLYN HUNT, *Raleigh*

# GOVERNOR HUNT'S FAVORITE HOLIDAY COOKIES

1½ cups sugar
1 cup butter, room temperature
2 eggs, beaten

3 cups flour
½ teaspoon baking soda
1 teaspoon vanilla

*Cream* sugar and butter well. Add eggs and beat. Add flour, baking soda and vanilla.

*Chill* 3 to 4 hours, then roll out and cut into ⅛-inch thick pieces. Bake at 350° F. until golden brown (about 8 to 10 minutes). Decorate with green and red sprinkles.

—GOVERNOR AND MRS. HUNT, *Raleigh*

*The most precious part of the holiday season is having our family together. We are extremely thankful for our health, our innumerable blessings, and that we have this time to gather together.*

—GOVERNOR JAMES B.
AND MRS. CAROLYN HUNT, *Raleigh*

the state: acorns, roses, juniper, amaryllis, hydrangeas, tobacco leaves, lemon leaves, brussels sprouts, birch bark, bittersweet, and holly. Perhaps the most spectacular display is the draperies in the library, which are made entirely of white pine and Fraser fir garlands with pine-cone cornices.

The second floor of the mansion is home to the first family of North Carolina. There, Governor and Mrs. Hunt celebrate Christmas with their children and grandchildren, wrap gifts, and bake sugar cookies.

The Executive Mansion in Raleigh belongs to all of the people of North Carolina, especially at Christmas.

*Gentlemen's parlor, the Executive Mansion*

# SOUTHERN SWEET POTATO CASSEROLE

6 medium sweet potatoes

1 ½ cups brown sugar

½ cup butter

½ cup milk

1 cup coconut

¼ teaspoon nutmeg

½ teaspoon cinnamon

marshmallows

*Boil, peel and mash* potatoes. Combine all ingredients except marshmallows. Place mixture in greased casserole dish and bake at 400° F. After 25 minutes, add marshmallows to the top and bake until golden brown.

—**GOVERNOR AND MRS. HUNT,** *Raleigh*

# PERSIMMON PUDDING

3 cups persimmon pulp

1 ½ cups brown sugar

1 cup sugar

1 medium raw sweet potato, grated

¾ cup flour

½ teaspoon baking powder

1 ½ cups buttermilk
(reserve 2 tablespoons)

1 teaspoon baking soda

1 teaspoon vanilla

1 cup sweet milk

3 eggs, beaten

1 stick butter, melted

*Preheat* oven to 325° F.

*Wash and sieve* persimmons to get pulp. Add brown sugar, sugar, potato, flour and baking powder to persimmon pulp. Mix the reserved buttermilk with the baking soda, then add the rest of the buttermilk and all other ingredients. Mix well. The mixture should resemble cake batter; if it is too thin add a little more flour.

*Pour* batter into well-greased 9x13-inch pan. Bake for 1 to 1 ½ hours, or until a toothpick inserted in center comes out clean.

*When cooled,* slice and serve with slightly sweetened whipped cream. Serves 10 to 12.

—**GOVERNOR AND MRS. HUNT,** *Raleigh*

*One of the Hunts' long-standing holiday traditions is to spend quality time with family, both immediate and extended. During this family time, it has been a custom that each family represented would provide some type of entertainment: singing, dancing, performing a pantomime, or playing musical instruments. When the children were small, they took piano or dance lessons, so they had an opportunity during this special time to share their talents with the extended family—grandparents, aunts, uncles, and cousins.*

—**GOVERNOR JAMES B. AND MRS. CAROLYN HUNT,** *Raleigh*

*Grandfather Mountain, as seen from MacRae Meadows, Avery County*

# Go Tell It on the Mountain

*(Traditional)*

To black slaves in the United States, the birth of a Savior who would set all men free was a miracle to be sung about. And when there was something so notable to tell, what better place to tell it from than a mountain, just as Jesus had chosen for His Sermon on the Mount. "Go Tell It on the Mountain," an authentic spiritual that dates probably from the early 1800s, was first popularized in 1879.

—READER'S DIGEST

Reprinted by permission from the *Reader's Digest Merry Christmas Songbook,* copyright © 1984. The Reader's Digest Association, Inc.

# Duke University Chapel

Come December, the joyous sounds of Christmas ring throughout the Duke University Chapel. Four organs (with more than 12,000 pipes), fifty carillon bells, and thousands of voices in dozens of choirs fill the building with song. Christmas concerts at the Duke University Chapel in Durham have been a beloved holiday tradition for decades. Special Christmas events include performances of Handel's "Messiah," concerts by the North Carolina Boys Choir, the Durham Civic Choral Society, the Duke Choral Society, and many chapel choirs.

In 1925, while planning the future site of the great university, founder James Buchanan Duke said to his friend, president William Preston Few, "I want the central building to be a church, a great towering church which will dominate all of the surroundings, because such an edifice would be bound to have a profound influence on the spiritual life of the young men and women who come here." The church was built in English gothic style with stone quarried from nearby Hillsborough. Seventy-seven stained-glass windows grace the chapel, fashioned from more than a million pieces of glass. Today the great towering church is an important center of activity for the university, Durham, and the surrounding communities.

Founded by Methodists, the Duke University Chapel is attended by peoples of many faiths, and numerous denominations hold Christmas services here, including the Roman Catholic, Episcopal, and Lutheran, among others. "These wonderful services are our gift to the community," says Will Willimon, Dean of the Chapel. "We welcome about six thousand people annually to our Christmas Eve services. They come from all the neighboring states as well to join us."

The Christmas Eve services have been a tradition at the chapel for more than twenty-five years. First is the children's service in the afternoon, followed by a communion service in the early evening. The candlelight service begins at 11:00 PM and is patterned after the service at King's College in Cambridge, England. It is a revered tradition here. In 1983 the temperature on Christmas Eve fell to below zero, yet the faithful still came, warming their spirits amid the shivering temperatures.

*Our Christmas season centers around family, friends, and church. Music is very important, and we are fortunate to be able to attend all the various services at the Duke University Chapel.*

**—MARY AND GEORGE PARKERSON,** *Durham*

Duke University Chapel, Durham

In December 1941, the Messiah Choir had just completed one of its Christmas concerts, and the resounding notes of the "Hallelujah" chorus were still ringing in the air. As people left the chapel, they noticed students huddled in cars, listening intently to their radios. It was December 7 and news reports had just announced the attack on Pearl Harbor. One young choir member knew his life would be changed forever. He joined the Marines, and several years later, while stationed on a remote island in the Pacific Ocean, he got word of the peace accords ending the war, once again to the inspiring music of the "Hallelujah" chorus.

—WILL WILLIMON, *Durham*

# Raleigh's Theatre in the Park

Charles Dickens's *A Christmas Carol* has delighted Raleigh audiences for more than twenty years. Theatre in the Park, North Carolina's largest community theater, begins the holiday festivities with its annual performances of this Christmas classic.

While the story may be an old favorite, there are always surprises in the Theatre in the Park's adaptation. Director Ira David Wood III, who also plays Ebeneezer Scrooge, follows about two-thirds of the story line of Dickens's traditional tale, but from there the performances takes twists and turns, and audiences never know whether Elvis Presley or Forrest Gump may appear! Since the script changes from year to year, performances never fail to be uproariously entertaining.

More than sixty members of the community take part in the production, with some actors as young as four. There are numerous sets and over a hundred costume changes. Attendance has topped the one-million mark, and the single largest audience numbered 10,000 people.

Another Theatre in the Park holiday favorite is *A Christmas Memory,* a one-man show about writer Truman Capote. Authorized by Capote, the play relives the heartwarming memories of his childhood Christmases. Company founder Ira David Wood III also stars in this production, poignantly portraying both Capote and the cousin who raised him.

Raleigh residents agree that Christmas would not be Christmas without the Theatre in the Park.

*ABOVE: A scene from the Theatre in the Park's annual production of Dickens's A Christmas Carol*

*RIGHT: Victorian carolers, North Carolina Zoo, Asheboro*

The Nutcracker, *presented at the J. E. Broyhill Civic Center, Caldwell County, by the Ballet Theatre of Pennsylvania*

*The annual performance of* The Nutcracker *was a special outing for our*
*family. Dressing up to go to Reynolds Auditorium was an event in itself for*
*the children, and they always looked like little sugarplum fairies themselves.*
*We still reminisce about those magical afternoons.*

—**MARY A. ALSPAUGH,** *Winston-Salem*

The all-volunteer Hickory Choral Society's annual
Christmas concert blends hundreds of voices with an
orchestra and guest soloists. This musical spectacular
draws sell-out crowds for every performance in
Hickory's Corinth Reformed United Church of Christ.

We always attend the Hickory Choral

Society Christmas Concert.

—DAVID AND SUSAN GUEST
Hickory

We play lots of special Christmas music during the holidays, but probably the favorite is "White Christmas" by Bing Crosby. All the kids have their own copies of the record, and while new versions come out every year, this one is always played over and over.

The big event is our "Christmas Band." Nearly everyone plays an instrument: oboe, flute, clarinets, guitar, piano, cornet, trombone, drums, and two bassoons. I have special arrangements and we play and sing everything we know until all our lips are worn out. Lots of fun!

—WILLIAM AND SARAH SPENCER, *Boone*

*Dressed in authentic Anglican-style vestments, the Boys' Choir of St. Peter's Episcopal Church, Charlotte, performs traditional Christmas music. During intermission, the boys change into jackets and ties to sing more contemporary selections.*

*North Carolina A&T State University Gospel Choir sings each year at Greensboro's renowned Festival of Lights, which includes the entire downtown area illuminated with lights.*

*From Thanksgiving to New Year's Eve, the North Carolina Symphony performs throughout the state, filling concert halls and auditoriums with beautiful holiday music.*

*The Marching Santas Band livens up the annual Christmas parade in West Jefferson, kicking off the Choose 'n Cut festivities in North Carolina's Fraser fir country.*

*Grassy Creek singing Christmas tree, Spruce Pine. The singers stand on elevated risers with a star at top.*

*Live musical presentations at Historic Malcolm Blue Farm, Aberdeen, entertain visitors at their holiday celebrations.*

*Historic Island Inn, Ocracoke*

# The Island Inn

Christmas at the historic Island Inn on Ocracoke is not an elaborate affair, but it
is warm and special. The inn, normally closed in winter, opens for a week from
December 26 through New Year's to host a gathering of guests—many of whom return
year after year—to thank them for their patronage and friendship. The inn is decorated
with both traditional holiday decorations and sea-related ornaments. Sand dollars and
seashells adorn the Christmas tree, and garlands of greenery are strung throughout the inn.

Built in 1901, this charming guest house on Silver Lake Harbor was originally an
Oddfellows Lodge. It has gone through several incarnations since then, including
the island's first public school, a private home, a coffee shop, and a naval officers' club.
Because most Ocracoke businesses close during the holidays, the Island Inn is an important
stop for locals and visitors celebrating the holiday season. The inn's fish and grits, an
Ocracoke staple for hundreds of years, is a favorite at Christmas and year round.

# ISLAND INN FISHCAKES

*At the Island Inn, we use red drum (channel bass) for fishcakes. We like yearling drum best. If drum is unavailable, you may use bluefish (but not the great big ones), trout, flounder or a combination. We serve our fishcakes with tartar sauce, green chili cheese grits, and, of course, cole slaw.*

1½ pounds fish fillets,
  skinned and boned

1 to 1½ pounds potatoes, peeled and
  diced into ⅓-inch cubes

1 small onion, chopped fine

¼ cup mayonnaise

2 tablespoons Dijon mustard

1 tablespoon Worchestershire sauce

1 tablespoon fresh lemon juice

2 tablespoons chopped, cooked bacon

¼ teaspoon cayenne pepper

½ teaspoon lemon pepper

dash of salt

dry bread crumbs

*Poach fish* in water until just cooked through. Drain well and flake into a large bowl. Boil potatoes in water until just fork tender, not mushy. Drain well. Add to fish. Add remaining ingredients except bread crumbs.

*Mix* together lightly. Use your hands to pat mixture into cakes, then roll cakes in bread crumbs to coat. At this point the fishcakes can be pan sautéd, fried lightly in oil, or frozen for a future date.

*Makes* approximately 12 to 15 3-ounce cakes.

—THE ISLAND INN, *Ocracoke*

---

## Sidebar

*Our favorite holiday tradition is decorating the inn, which always culminates with a tree trimming party in the lobby parlor.*

—CLAUDIA AND BOB TOUHY
*Innkeepers, The Island Inn*

---

# GREEN CHILI CHEESE GRITS CASSEROLE

1 cup regular grits or quick grits
  (not instant)

½ teaspoon salt

3 cups boiling water

3 eggs, beaten

1 cup milk

2 tablespoons melted butter

½ cup shredded cheddar cheese

1 small can chopped green chilis
  (jalapeños or other hot peppers
  may be substituted)

1 teaspoon minced garlic

dash of pepper

*Preheat* oven to 350° F.

*Add* grits and salt to boiling water. Boil over low heat until smooth. Remove from heat. Add eggs to milk and butter, and stir into grits. Add cheese, chilis, garlic and pepper. Mix gently. Pour into casserole.

*Bake* for 30 to 40 minutes, or until just beginning to brown.

—THE ISLAND INN, *Ocracoke*

since 1901

*Father Christmas, the Southern Christmas Show, Charlotte*

*I always remember going to Dr. E. T. Beddingfield's*

*New Year's Eve Christmas tree burning in Stantonsberg.*

**—BILL PITTMAN,** *Wilson*

## New Year's Roast Pork and Sauerkraut

*This dish is* a must *to bring good luck for the coming year.*

Pork roast
Sauerkraut

*Place* pork roast in slow cooker with kraut spread over the top. Let cook slowly all night and all the next day until ready for dinner. The longer it is cooked the better. Serve with cornbread.

—**Judy Rupard,** *Elk Park*

*There's a big community barbecue near where we live, and we always go at Christmastime.*

—**Anonymous,** *Concord*

## Cabbage and Black-eyed Peas with Streaked Meat

Cabbage
Black-eyed peas

Streaked meat
*(fat back or a leaner cut if you prefer)*

*Boil* cabbage with black-eyed peas and serve with cooked streaked meat.

*Grandma and Grandpa owned the Tatem Hotel in Elk Park when the railroad came through town, and they served this at New Year's for good luck.*

—**Judy Rupard,** *Elk Park*

*Our family and friends always ate black-eyed peas on New Year's because it was supposed to bring you money in the following year. If you didn't eat black-eyed peas, you would be in danger of financial trouble during the year.*

—**Ruby McSwain,** *Sanford*

## Barbecued Pigs Feet

5 large pigs feet (halves)
4 celery sprigs
2 bay leaves
2 tablespoons vinegar
1 15-ounce can of tomato sauce

1 large onion, sliced
1 tablespoon salt
1 teaspoon pepper
2 cups barbecue sauce

*In a large pot,* cover pigs feet with water. Add rest of ingredients except for barbecue sauce. Boil until pigs feet are tender.

*Place* pigs feet in a large baking pan and pour a cup of stock from the pot over the pigs feet and add the barbecue sauce. Brown in a 350° F. oven for approximately 30 to 35 minutes. Baste twice during browning time.

—**Lillie S. Cuthrell,** *Winston-Salem*

*OPPOSITE: Fraser firs, Mount Mitchell State Park, Yancey County*

# Holiday Events

**Aberdeen**
Malcolm Blue Farm Open House
*Second week in December*

**Albemarle**
An Albemarle Downtown Christmas
*End of November*

**Allegheny County**
Christmas Tree Growers' Assn.
Choose 'n Cut
*First weekend in December*

Christmas Craft Fair
*Saturday after Thanksgiving*

**Apex**
Christmas Historic Homes Tour
*First Sunday in December*

Christmas Tree Lighting Ceremony
*First Friday in December*

Christmas Parade through
Historic Downtown
*First Saturday in December*

**Asheboro**
Christmas at the Zoo
*Three days in mid-December*

**Asheville**
A Grove Park Inn Christmas
*Thanksgiving through New Year's*

Annual Christmas Parade
*Friday after Thanksgiving*

Asheville Symphony Messiah
Sing-Along
*Last week in November*

Annual High Country Christmas
Art and Craft Show.
*Last week in November*

Christmas Greens Market
*Three Saturdays in December*

Dickens in the Village,
at Biltmore Village
*First week in December*

Reindeer Romp 5K Fun Run
and 1-Mile Walk
*First week in December*

Children's Festival
*First week in December*

African Holiday Expo
*First week in December*

Hanukkah Celebration of Lights
*First week in December*
Kwanzaa, an African-American
Celebration
*December 27*

First Night Asheville
*December 31*

Christmas at Biltmore Estate
*November and December*

Christmas at the
Smith–McDowell House
*Thanksgiving through
New Year's Eve*

Return to Bethlehem:
A Journey of the Heart
*First week in December*

Thomas Wolfe Memorial
Christmas Tours
*Three weeks in December*

Vance Birthplace Candlelight Tours
and Open House
*Three weeks in December*

UNCA Holiday Concert
*First week in December*

"The Nutcracker" Ballet
*Early December*

Asheville Symphony Holiday Concert
*Third week of December*

**Bailey**
Holidays at the Country Doctor Museum
*First week in December*

**Beaufort**
Beaufort by the Sea Christmas, including
arrival of Santa by boat
*Saturday after Thanksgiving*

**Beech Mountain**
North Pole at Beech
*Third week in December*

**Black Mountain**
Black Mountain Christmas Parade and
Community Candle Lighting
*First Saturday in December*

**Blowing Rock**
Lighting of the Town
*Friday after Thanksgiving*

Tellabration Storytelling Festival
*Friday before Thanksgiving*

Old Fashioned Christmas
*Thanksgiving through
New Year's Eve*

Christmas in the Park, with bonfire and
Mr. & Mrs. Claus
*Friday after Thanksgiving*
Christmas Parade
*Saturday after Thanksgiving*

Hometown Holidays Variety Show
*Saturday after Thanksgiving*

Christmas Concert,
Watauga Community Band
*First Saturday in December*

Annual Community Advent Walk
*First week in December*

Gingerbread House Competition and
Exhibit
*First two weeks in December*

New Year's Eve Celebration
at Appalachian Ski Mountain
*December 31*

**Boone**
Olde Boone Christmas Parade
*First week in December*

Olde Boone Christmas Celebration
*Three weekends in December*

Stages of the Nativity
in Boone Churches.
*Second week in December*

Santa at Sugar Mountain
*Last week before Christmas*

Ski Hawksnest
New Year's Celebration
*December 31*

**Brevard**
Festival of Trees
*First week in December*

Twilight Tour on Main Street
*First Saturday in December*

**Bryson City**
Merchants Christmas Parade
*First Saturday in December*

**Burke County**
Western Carolina Center Christmas Parade
*First Thursday after Thanksgiving*

Holiday Show and Sale
*Second week in November*

**Burlington**
Winter Wonderland
*Second week in November*

Holiday Craft Show
*Third week in November*

Holiday Pops Concert,
North Carolina Symphony
*Late November or December*

Christmas Homes Tour
and Candlelight Tea
*First week in December*

Christmas Tea at the Carousel
*Second week in December*

18th-Century Christmas
Celebration at Alamance Battleground
State Historic Site
*Second week in December*

**Caldwell County**
Annual Christmas Craft Show,
Caldwell County Fairgrounds
*Second week in November*

Hudson Tree Lighting and Arrival of Santa
*December 1*

Lenoir Christmas Parade
*First Saturday in December*

Sawmills Christmas Parade
*First Saturday in December*

Granite Falls Christmas Parade
*First Saturday in December*

Hudson Christmas Parade
*First Saturday in December*

The Singing Tree,
J.E. Broyhill Civic Center
*First Saturday in December*

Fort Defiance's
An Old Fashioned Christmas
*First Sunday afternoon in December*

J.E. Broyhill Civic Center,
Christmas programs and play.
*Throughout December*

**Cameron**
Christmas Open House
*Week before Thanksgiving*

Christmas Lighting
*Second week in December*

**Carolina Beach**
Christmas Parade
*First Saturday in December*

Island of Lights Lighting
*Saturday after Thanksgiving*

Island of Lights Flotilla
*First week in December*

Island of Lights Homes Tour
*Second week in December*

Island of Lights
New Year's Eve Celebration.
*December 31*

**Carthage**
Christmas Open House, The Bryant
House and McLendon Cabin
*Second week in December*

House in the Horseshoe
Open House
*Second week in December*

**Chapel Hill**
Star of Bethlehem
at Moorehead Planetarium
*Mid-November through mid-January*

Community Sing and Tree Lighting
*First week in December*

**Charlotte**
Christmas Made in the South Craft Show.
*Third week in October*

Southern Christmas Show
*Mid-November*

Back Country Christmas:
Historic Latta Plantation
*Late November and
early December*

Carolina Country Christmas Classic
*Weekend after Thanksgiving*

Christmas Parade
*Thanksgiving Day*

"A Christmas Carol"
*Two weekends in December*

Lighting Downtown
*First week in December*

Children's Theatre Supper
with Santa
*First weekend in December*

Gnomes at Christmas
*Second week in December*

Holiday Storytelling
*Mid-December*

Moravian Love Feast
at Queens College
*First week in December*

Charlotte Symphony
Holiday Concert
*Second week in December*

Singing Christmas Tree
*Second week in December*

Handel's "Messiah"
*One weekend in December*

First Night Charlotte
*December 31*

**Clemmons**
Tanglewood Festival of Lights
*Mid-November through mid-January*
Holiday Pops Concert,
North Carolina Symphony
*End of November*

**Cleveland County** *(See also Shelby)*
King's Mountain Christmas Parade
*First week in December*
Christmas Home Tour,
King's Mountain
*Thanksgiving through third week
in December*

Christmas of Wildlife,
King's Mountain State Park
*Third week in December*

Love Light Ceremony, Lawndale
*First week in December*

**Clinton**
Holiday Pops Concert,
North Carolina Symphony
*Early November or December*

**Concord**
Concord Christmas and
Candlelight Tour
*First week in December*

**Dallas** *(See Gaston County)*

**Denton**
Christmas Home Tours
*Second week in December*

Holiday Musical
*Mid-December*

**Drexel**
Singing Christmas Tree
*First week in December*

**Dunn Area**
Community Tree Lighting,
Open House, and Arrival of Santa
*First week in December*

Dunn Christmas Parade
*First week in December*

**Durham**
Durham Holiday Parade and Festival
*Sunday before Thanksgiving*

Handel's "Messiah,"
Duke University Chapel
*First week in December*

Festival of Trees,
American Red Cross
*First week in December*

Bennett Place Christmas Open House
*First week in December*

Stagville Center State Historic Site
Christmas Open House
*First week in December*

Holiday Pops Concert,
Durham Symphony
*Late November or December*

Christmas Concert, Duke University
Department of Music
*Second week in December*

Home for the Holidays, Duke
Homestead State Historic Site
*Second week in December*

Christmas Concert,
Durham Civic Choral Society
*Second weekend in December*

Christmas at West Point,
Eno City Park
*Second week in December*

Christmas by Candlelight,
Duke Homestead
*Second week in December*

Christmas Tours for Children,
Duke Homestead
*Second week in December*

Santa Train, Museum of Life
and Science
*Third week in December*

**Edenton**
Christmas in Historic Edenton James
Iredell House
*Mid-December*

**Elizabeth City**
Museum of the Albemarle
Christmas Open House,
Down on the Farm Christmas
*First week in November*

Holiday Celebration
and Lighted Boat Parade
*Sunday after Thanksgiving*

Christmas at the Art Gallery.
*Early December*

Christmas Parade
*Early December*

Christmas Theatre
*Early December*

**Fayetteville**
Holly Day Fair
*First week in November*

Holiday Pops Concert,
North Carolina Symphony.
*Late November or December*

Eastern Carolina Craftsmen's Christmas
Festival
*Last week in November*

Singing Christmas Tree
*First week in December*

Christmas Craft Fair, Fort Bragg
*First week in December*

Christmas Pageant,
Cape Fear Regional Theatre
*Mid-December*

Christmas Candlelight Tours
*Second week in December*

Christmas on Heritage Square,
Fayetteville
*Second week in December*

Christmas Pops Concert, Fayetteville
Symphony Orchestra
*Early December*

Santa's Workshop and Express
*Mid December*

**Flat Rock**
Christmas in Connemara, Carl
Sandburg's House Historic Site
*Four weekends between
Thanksgiving and Christmas*

Blue Ridge Christmas Celebration
*Second week in December*

**Fort Bragg** *(See Fayetteville)*

**Franklin**
Celebration on the Square
*First week in December*

**Fremont**
Governor Charles B. Aycock
Birthplace Candlelight Tours
*Mid-December*

**Garner**
Christmas Parade
*First week in December*

Land of Fantasy
*Mid-November through
first week in January*

**Gaston County**
Crowders Mountain Fall Festival,
Crowders Mountain State Park
*November*

Harvest Day, Schiele Museum
*November*

Christmas Town U.S.A.
Tree and Light Showing, McAdenville
*December 1 through December 26*

Christmas in the City,
Downtown Gastonia
*December*

Celebrate with Wildlife,
Schiele Museum
*December*

Dickens of a Christmas, Gaston County
Museum of Art & History
*December*

Colonial Christmas,
Schiele Museum
*December*

Toys Were Us, Gaston County Museum
of Art & History
*December*

A Garden's Harvest, Daniel Stowe
Botanical Garden
*December*

**Georgeville**
Reed Gold Mine Christmas Celebration
*First week in December*

**Granville County/Oxford**
Santa's Arrival—Lighting of the Greens in
Historic Oxford
*Friday after Thanksgiving*

Christmas Parade
*First Sunday in December*

Christmas Tour of Homes
*Second Sunday in December*

Creedmoor Christmas Parade
*First Saturday in December*

Butner Christmas Parade
*First Saturday in December*

Grassy Creek Christmas Parade
*Second Saturday in December*

**Goldsboro**
"The Nutcracker"
*First week in December*

Oratorio Christmas Concert
*First week in December*

Holiday Market and
Christmas Concerts
*November and December*

Boychoir Christmas Concert
*Mid-December*

**Greensboro**
Christmas at Market Square
*Mid-November*

Celebrating Native Americans
of the Piedmont.
*Mid-November*

Wassail Tea
*Mid-November*

Carolina Craftsmen's Christmas Classic
*Last week in November*

Moravian Candle Tea
*First weekend in December*

Festival of Lights
*First weekend in December*

Guilford College Choir Concert
*First week in December*

The "Messiah," by Greensboro Oratorio
Society
*First week in December*

"The Nutcracker"
*Second weekend in December*

Christmas at the Carolin.
*Second weekend in December*

Candlefest (Luminaries)
*Second Sunday in December*

Christmas Open House
*Second Sunday in December*

Living Christmas Tree,
Greensboro Choral Society
*Mid-December*

Greensboro Symphony
Christmas Concert.
*Mid-December*

"A Christmas Carol"
*Third week in December*

**Havelock**
Christmas in the Park
*Mid-December*

Henderson and Vance County
Community Tree Lighting
*Late November*

Vance United in Song,
Christmas Concert
*Early December*

Christmas Parade
*Early December*

**Hendersonville**
The "Messiah"
*First week in December*

Christmas Concert
*Second week in December*

Festival of Lights
*Mid-December*

**Hickory**
Christmas in the Valley
Craft Show
*Thanksgiving weekend*

Hickory Choral Society Concert
*First weekend in December*

Western Piedmont Symphony
Festival of Trees
*December*

**High Point**
Lilliputian Christmas,
Peterson Doll Museum
*Through December*

"A Christmas Carol," by North Carolina
Shakespeare Festival
*Two weekends in December*

High Point Museum
Christmas Open House
*First week in December*

First Night Piedmont
*December 31*

**Hillsborough**
Christmas Candlelight Tour
*First week in December*

**Holly Ridge**
Holly Festival
*First Saturday in November*

**Huntersville**
Backcountry Christmas
at Historic Latta Place
*Last weekend in November*

**Jacksonville**
Twelve Days of Christmas
*Sunday after Thanksgiving and
two weeks in December*

Christmas Tree Lighting and Flotilla
*First Saturday in December*

Holiday Parade
*Saturday before Thanksgiving*

**Kannapolis**
Annual Christmas Parade
*Tuesday after Thanksgiving*

Christmas in the Village
*End of November through
Christmas Eve*

**Kenansville**
Candlelight Christmas
at Liberty Hall
*Second week in December*

**Kenly**
Christmas Open House
*First week in December*

Christmas Story Nativity
*Last weekend before Christmas*

Christmas Open House at the Tobacco
Farm Life Museum
*First weekend in December*

**Lexington Area**
Uptown Christmas Open House
*Sunday before Thanksgiving*

Night of Lights
*Sunday after Thanksgiving*

Christmas Candlelight Service
*First week in December*

Christmas Parade
*First week in December*

Christmas on the Square
*First week in December*

Community Carol Sing
*Second week in December*

A Night of Candlelight and Carols
*Mid-December*

**Lincolnton**
Holiday Pops Concert,
North Carolina Symphony
*Late November or December*

**Matthews**
Victorian High Tea
in Historic Reid House
*First two weekends in December*

**Mitchell County**
Bethlehem Marketplace
*First weekend in December*

Animal Shelter Annual
Christmas Bazaar
*First Saturday in December*

Christmas Ornament Show,
Twisted Laurel Gallery
*Thanksgiving through
New Year's Eve*

Christmas Program Presented
by the Children of the YMCA
*Middle of December*

Parade of Lights
*First Saturday in December*

**Montgomery County**
Christmas Tree Lighting in Troy
and Arrival of Santa.
*Wednesday before Thanksgiving*

Star Christmas Parade and
Miss Merry Christmas Contest
*Second Saturday in December*

**Moorehead City**
Holiday Pops Concert,
North Carolina Symphony
*Late November or December*

**Mount Airy**
Victorian Christmas Open House
*Selected days throughout December*

Christmas Holiday Tour of Homes
*Second weekend in December*

Children's Theatre
*Mid-December*

Moravian Love Feast
*Christmas Eve*

**Mount Olive Area**
Christmas Pops Concert,
North Carolina Symphony
*Late November or December*

Christmas Tree Lighting,
Town Square
*First Friday in December*

Christmas Parade
*First Saturday in December*

**Murfreesboro**
Holiday Pops Concert,
North Carolina Symphony
*Late November or December*

**New Bern**
Holiday Showcase
*Day after Thanksgiving
through Christmas Eve*

Holiday Tour of Historic Bed and
Breakfast Inns
*First Sunday in December*

Coastal Christmas Flotilla and Parade
*First Saturday in December*

Tryon Palace Historic Sites
and Gardens Christmas
*First through third week
in December*

Tryon Palace, Candlelight Tours
*First two weekends in December*

**Newton**
Christmas Tree Lighting
*Day after Thanksgiving*

Lighting of the Luminaries
*First Sunday in December*

**Oak Island**
Christmas by the Sea Festival Parade
*First Saturday in December*

Beautification Club Tour of Homes
*First Sunday in December*

**Old Fort**
Old Mountain Christmas
*Three weekends in December*

**Oriental**
Spirit of Christmas
*Second week in December*

**Oxford** *(See Granville County)*

**Pinehurst**
Holiday Pops Concert,
North Carolina Symphony
*Late November or December*

Christmas Through the Ages
*December 1 through Christmas Eve*

Christmas Tree Lighting
*First Friday in December*

Village Festivities
*December through Christmas Eve*

Moore County Choral
Society Christmas Concert
*First weekend in December*

Holiday Concert
*Second week in December*

**Pineville**
18th-Century Christmas at
James K. Polk Historic Site
*First week in December*

**Raleigh Area**
"A Christmas Carol,"
Theatre In The Park
*Mid-December*

A Carolina Christmas Show
*Mid-November*

Land of Fantasy, Animated Drive
Light Spectacular, Walnut Creek
Amphitheater
*Mid-November through first
week in January*

Raleigh's Annual Christmas Parade
*Saturday before Thanksgiving*

Carolina Designer Craftsmen Annual Fair
*Thanksgiving weekend*

Holidays Pops Concert,
North Carolina Symphony
*Thanksgiving weekend*

Go Naturally for the Holidays, North
Carolina State Museum of Natural Sciences
*Thanksgiving through
New Year's Eve*

Annual Madrigal Dinner
*Late November through
early December*

Fuquay-Varina Christmas Tree Lighting
Ceremony
*First week in December*

"Messiah" Sing-In, with Raleigh
Symphony Orchestra and National
Opera Company
*First week in December*

Dickens Fair
*First week in December*

Moravian Candle Tea
*First week in December*

North Carolina Museum
of Art Holiday Family Festival
*First week in Decembe*

North Carolina Museum of
History Di Yiddishe Band Concert
*Early December*

Walk-in Workshop
*First week in December*

Walk-in Workshop:
Moravian Christmas
*Second week in December*

Family Night: Prepare to Celebrate!
*Mid-December*

Knightdale Christmas Parade
*First week in December*

Cary Holiday Tree Lighting
and Open House
*First Sunday in December*

"Messiah," Cary Community Choir
*First Sunday in December*

Meredith College Christmas Concert.
*First Sunday in December*

Morrisville Christmas Tree Lighting and
Cantata Ceremony
*First Sunday in December*

Zebulon Christmas Parade
*First Sunday in December*

Lighting of the Wendell Town Square
*First week in December*

Apex Historical Society's Christmas
Homes Tour
*Early December*

Apex Christmas Parade
*First week in December*

Week of Giving. State Farmers Market
*First week in December*

Peace College Annual
Christmas Concert
*First weekend in December*

Executive Mansion Holiday
Open House
*Early December*

Lighting of the Grove,
Saint Mary's College
*Second week in December*

Fuquay–Varina Christmas Parade
*Mid-December*

Governor's State Tree
Lighting Celebration
*Early December*

Annual Living Christmas Tree
*Second week in December*

Spirit of Christmas Past at Mordecai
Historic Park,
*Last three weeks of December*

A Raleigh Christmas Celebration,
Providence Baptist Church
*Second week in December*

Haywood Hall Open House
*Second weekend in December*

Twelve Days of Christmas,
State Capitol
*Mid-December*

Historic Oakwood Candlelight Tour
*Mid-December*

North Carolina State University
Christmas Concert
*Mid-December*

"The Nutcracker" Ballet, North Carolina
Symphony and North Carolina School of
the Arts
*Third week in December*

Raleigh Flute Choir
Annual Holiday Concert
*Mid-December*

"A Christmas Memory,"
Theatre in the Park
*Mid-December*

Holiday Concert, Raleigh Concert Band
and St. Raphael Choir
*Mid-December*

Joel Lane Christmas Open House.
*Mid-December*

Christmas Concert, Concert Singers of Cary
*Mid-December*

Raleigh Boychoir
*Late December*

Viennese New Year's Eve Concert,
North Carolina Symphony
*December 31*

First Night Raleigh with North Carolina
Symphony Family Concert
*December 31*

Kwanzaa
*Late December*

**Reidsville**
Chinqua-Penn Plantation
Holiday Tours
*Month of December*

**Roanoke Rapids**
Holiday Pops Concer.
*Late November or December*

**Rodanthe**
Christmas with Old Buck
*January 6*

**Rocky Mount**
Christmas Tree Decoration
*Sunday after Thanksgiving*

Festival of Trees
*Wednesday after Thanksgiving*

Arts Center Christmas Concert
*First week in December*

Arts Center Winter Craft Bazaar
*Saturday before Thanksgiving*

**Salisbury**
Christmas Crafts Festival
*Third week in November*

Christmas in Historic
Downtown Salisbury.
*Thanksgiving through Christmas Eve*

Christmas Cheer Concert
*First week in December*

Victorian Christmas at Hall House
*Three weekends in December*

**Sedalia**
Charlotte Hawkins Brown Memorial
Christmas Open House
*Second week in December*

**Shelby**
Holiday Carriage Rides
*Four weeks in November
and December*

City Hall Tree Lighting
*First week in December*

**Smithfield**
Christmas Festival
*First week in December*

**Snow Hill**
Holiday Pops Concert
*Late November or December*

**Southern Pines**
Weymouth Christmas House
*First week in December*

Historic Christmas Open Houses
*Early December*

Tree Lighting
*First weekend in December*

Candlelight Tour
*Second weekend in December*

Sandhills Horticultural Gardens
Open House
*Second weekend in December*

Christmas Horse Carriage Drive
*Third Saturday in December*

**Southport**
Southport Home Tour
*Second week in December*

Port Charlies Holiday Boat Flotilla.
*Early December*

**Sparta**
Christmas Parade
*Saturday after Thanksgiving*

Choose and Cut Day.
*First week in December*

**Spencer**
North Carolina Transportation
Museum Holiday
*Thanksgiving through third week
in December*

**Statesville**
Christmas Past Revisited
*First weekend in December*

Christmas at the Cabins
*First week in December*

Handel's Walk-in "Messiah"
*First week in December*

**Swansboro**
Holiday Flotilla
*Saturday after Thanksgiving*

**Thomasville**
Light Up Your Holidays
*Third week in November*

**Troy** *(See Montgomery County)*

**Valdese**
"A Christmas Carol"
*Two weekends in December*

**Wake Forest**
Wake Forest Christmas Tour
*First week in December*

Lighting of Wake Forest
*First week in December*

**Washington**
Yuletide by the Riverside
*First week in December*

**Waynesville**
Historic Waynesville Holiday
Homes Tour
*First week in December*

Breakfast with Santa
*Two Saturdays in December*

"The Nutcracker"
*Second week in December*

**Weaverville** *(See Asheville)*

**Webster**
Christmas in Webster
*Two Saturdays in December*

**West Jefferson**
Choose and Cut Weekend and Parade
*First weekend in December*

Ashe County Choral Society Holiday
Concert
*First week in December*

Christmas Tour of Homes
*First week in December*

**Whiteville**
Holidays Pops Concert,
North Carolina Symphony
*Late November or December*

**Wilkesboro**
Appalachian Craft Show
*First week in November*

Holiday Pops Concert,
North Carolina Symphony
*Late November or December*

Wilkes Christmas Parade
*First week in December*

Holiday Home Tour
*Second weekend of December*

North Carolina Children's Concert
*First week in December*

Arrival of Santa Claus
*First weekend in December*

Wilkes Playmaker
*First week in December*

**Wilmington**
Festival of Trees and Children's
Festival Land
*Thanksgiving through first week
in December*

Illumination of Riverfront Park
*Friday after Thanksgiving*

Henrietta II Holiday Cruises
*Three weeks in December and
New Year's Eve*

Old Wilmington by Candlelight
and Wassail Bowl
*First week in December*

Tree-Lighting Ceremony and
Santa's House
*Two weeks in December*

Poplar Grove Christmas Celebration
*First week in December*

Walk-in "Messiah"
*First week in December*

*USS North Carolina* Battleship
Memorial Christmas Decorations
*Second week in December through
first week in January*

Holidays Pops Concert,
North Carolina Symphony
*Late November or December*

Caroling by Carriage
*Mid-December*

**Wilson**
Holiday Pops Concert,
North Carolina Symphony
*Late November or December*

Downtown Wilson Lights Up
*Weekend before Thanksgiving*

Christmas Parade
*Sunday after Thanksgiving*

Downtown Carriage Rides with Santa
and Mrs. Claus
*Three days in December*

A Banker's Holiday
*Second Friday after Thanksgiving*

Santa's Workshop and Toys for Tots.
*Three days in December*

White's Lights
*Second week in December
through Christmas night*

*Miracle on Nash Street*
*First week in December*

Candlelight Tours,
Gov. Charles B. Aycock Birthplace
*Second week in December*

Christmas Fantasy,
Imagination Station
Science Museum
*Tuesday after Thanksgiving*

'Twas the Flight Before Christmas,
Imagination Station
Science Museum
*Third week in December*

**Windsor**
Christmas at Hope Plantation, tours of
Hope Mansion and King-Blazemore House
*Second Sunday in December
through December 20*

**Winston-Salem**
Tanglewood Festival of Lights
*Mid-November to mid-January*

Christmas Tree Lighting
*First week in December*

Historic Bethabara Christmas,
with Moravian Music Foundation
*November and December*

Old Salem Christmas at Restored
Moravian Village
*Throughout December*

Holiday Parade
*Saturday after Thanksgiving*

"Messiah" Community Concert
*First week in December*

Deck the Hall Holiday Sale
of Arts and Crafts
*First week in December*

"The Nutcracker" Ballet
*First week in December*

Candle Tea
*November and December*

Candlelight Tours at Gemeinhaus
*Early December*

Reynolda House and Graylyn Conference
Center Open House
*Second week in December*

"A Christmas Carol," North Carolina
Shakespeare Festival
*Mid-December*

Moravian Love Feast
*Christmas Eve*

First Night Celebration
*December 31*

**Wrightsville Beach**
Light Up the Beach
*Thanksgiving through
New Year's Day*

North Carolina Holiday Flotilla
*Saturday after Thanksgiving*

**Yanceyville**
Historic Homes Tour
*First week in December*

Christmas Parade
*First week in December*

## PHOTO CREDITS

Acker, John (Greensboro
  Preservation Society) 29 (bottom)
Battleship *North Carolina*, Inc., 53
  (Printed with permission.)
Bengtson, Lena, 63 (bottom)
Biltmore Estate, Inc., The, 66
  (top, bottom), 67, 68
Caldwell County Historical
  Society, 52
Chinqua-Penn Foundation, Inc., 73
Clarke, Brian S., 113 (bottom right)
Connan, Bob (Fearrington/Fitch
  Creations), 27 (bottom)
Crosby, David, 12 (top, bottom),
  16 (top, bottom), 17, 21, 24-25,
  26 (top), 28, 30, 34, 37, 41, 45
  (top, bottom left, bottom right),
  57, 58 (top, bottom), 59, 61, 62
  (top), 63, 64-65, 69, 77, 78 (top,
  bottom), 80 (top, bottom), 82, 83
  (top, bottom), 84 (top, bottom),
  85, 86, 89, 93 (bottom), 94, 98,
  100, 111, 112 (top), 113 (top),
  114 (top), 117, 124 (top), Inside
  Back/Jacket
DeVita, Debbie, 124 (bottom)
Holt, Dave (Eastern National Park
  & Monuments Association), 56
Graue, David, 55 (top)
Grove Park Inn, The, 92 (top,
  bottom), 93 (top)
Gumbs & Thomas Publishers, Inc., 88
Hamilton, Marcus, 54 (lower left,
  lower right)
Harris, Brownie, 31 (top)
Harris, Marty, 115
Hilliard, Mary, 46 (top, bottom),
  47 (top, bottom)
Hope Plantation Foundation, Inc., 50
Humphries, George, front cover,
  1, 2, 4-5, 9, 14, 48-49, 51, 74-75,
  76, 90-91, 106, 119
Hunt, Jim, 54 (top)
Island of Lights Committee, 31
  (lower right)
Jones, Charles E., (State Photographer,
  North Carolina DOT), 103 (top,
  bottom), 104-105
Kiefer, Jan, 87
May, Kelly (Burlington/Alamance),
  27 (top)
McAdenville, Christmas Town USA,
  31 (lower left)
Mitchell County Chamber of
  Commerce, 114 (lower left)
Morris, Dick (Matthews Historical
  Foundation) 29 (top)
North Carolina Christmas Tree
  Association, 18, 19, 20, 23
North Carolina Symphony, 112-113
North Carolina Zoo, 110 (bottom)
Peersen, Olve 26 (bottom)
Pinehurst Convention & Visitors'
  Bureau, 101, 114 (lower right)
Richmond Hill Inn, 7, 32, 33
Scancarelli, Jim, 55 (bottom)
Spoon, Janet, 62 (bottom)
Theatre in the Park, 110 (top)
Thomas, Bernard, 108-109
Williams, Jack (Chowan County), 71
Winston-Salem Convention and
  Visitors' Bureau-Old Salem, 10, 11

## GEORGE HUMPHRIES

Nature photographer George Humphries won critical acclaim—and a loyal following—with the publication of his bestselling book, *North Carolina, Images of Wildness* (Westcliffe Publishers), now in its third printing. Also published as notecards and calendars, his photographs capture the scenic beauty of North Carolina—at Christmastime and throughout the year. A high school history teacher, George lives in Asheville with his wife, Linda, and their three children, Katie, Sean, and Weston.

## DAVID CROSBY

An award-winning commercial photographer, David Crosby specializes in showing the human side of a high-tech world. David, who opened his studio eleven years ago, also teaches photography and has had his fine art work displayed regionally. A graduate of Duke University, he lives in Hickory with his wife, Joy, and their two children, Laurel and John.

*We would like to extend our deep appreciation to the Grove Park Inn Resort, Asheville, for graciously offering their facilities and the services of their staff to assist in several food shots included in this book.*

*Both George Humphries and David Crosby maintain stock photo libraries. For more information, contact Westcliffe Publishers.*

# Thank You, North Carolina

John Acker
Robert K. Akins
Lucy Allen
Wilson Angley
Antioch Baptist Church
Vicky Alexander
Lucy Allen
Meredith Allsopp
Mary Alspaugh
Luther Ashby
Carla Ashton
Ballet Theater
  of Pennsylvania
Bank of Granite
Paulina Barney
Jennifer Barnhart
Melinda Barth
Margaret Bell
Lena Bengtson
Ronnie Berndt
Dottie and Bobby Berry
Julie Bledsoe
Carrie Lee Booth
Arvis Boughman
Boys' Choir of St. Peters
  Episcopal Church,
  Ben Outen, Music
  Director
Barbara Bradshaw
David Briggs
Eric Bright
Lisa W. Briley
Greg Browsteen
Kathy Bryan
Elizabeth Bruton
Michelle Burgess
Jerry Burns
Carla Carrick
Jenny Case
Jerry Cashion
Catawba County
  Historical Association
Steven Catlett
Knight Chamberlain
Chetola Estates
Melissa Christian
Mary Clark
Brian S. Clarke
Louann Clarke
Michelle Clifton
Dale Coates
Vicki Coggins
Carlton Cook
Charles E.
  and Nancy Cordell
Al Corum
Bernice Couch
Burnette B. Covington
April Cox
Sue Cozart
Betty Crawford
Rev. Dr. Robert H.
  Crewdson
Joy, Laurel, and John Crosby
Lillie S. Cuthrell
Angie Daniels
Berry Davidson
Kathryn Davis
Fred Dawi

Will Deal
Thomas A. Devine
Debbie DeVita
Glenda Dills
Dona Dyche
Don Edwards
Betty Eidenier
Mary Elder
Jan Ellington
Tim S. Elliott
Linda Eure
Jane Fairbanks
Carol Field
Mark File
Fort Defiance, Inc.
Kerri Fraley
Joni Fredman
Fred's Mercantile Store
William Friday
Gail Fripp
Susan, Joshua, Samantha,
  and Jennifer Frost
Margaret Fuller
Dot Fuss
Sandra D. Gambill
Jay Garner
Susan George
Thelma George
Linda Georgitis
Karen Gibbs
Carol Gilliam
Clifford and
  Maybelle Glenn
Leonard and Clara Glenn
Sue Glovier
Golden Shears
Casey Goodwin
David Graue
Mary Greene
Jeanne Griffin
Susan and David Guest
Marcus Hamilton
Ellen Hardy
Esther Harmon
Rachel Harmon
Brownie Harris
Charlotte Hartley
John O. Hawkins
David Heavener
Tim Helms
Bruce Hetcher
Hickory Choral Society,
  Don Coleman, Creative
  Director
Hickory Landmarks
  Society, Claire Bost
Beth Highley
Marie Hogan
Glenda Hayes Holaday
Gloria Houston
Nettie Howell
Linda Humphries
Jim Hunt
Governor James B. and
  Mrs. Carolyn Hunt
Dean and Dottie Illig
Faye Inman
Richard C. Jackson
Sharon Kellam

Carolyn Ketchum
Melissa Kiefer
Joyce Knabb
Deb Konezal
Charlotte Kraay
Ken Kraay
Wes & Jewel Kraay
Nora Kuester
Jim, Trish, Molly, and
  Jimmy Lancaster
Peggy Langley
Judith Langston
Henry Lathan
Gina Lathum
Mr. Lazenby
Hans J. Lenz
Jane Lieberman
Robin Lindsey
Barbara Locklear
Naomi Long
Vickie Long
Clarice Lopp
Bobbie Ludgin
Archie Lynch
Cy Lynn
Christ Mackey
Melissa Mankowski
Rhonda B. Martin
Kelly G. May
Kathleen McArthur
Sue McDonough
Ken McFarland
Bobbie McIntosh
Linda Medford
Zoraya Mendez-DeCosmis
Patty Meredith
Diane Messick
Debbi Miles
Edna Miller,
  Miller's Tree Farm
Joy Minton
Jodee Mitchell
Jean A. Moore
Rebecca Moore
Eleanor and Dick Morris
Jeanette Morton
Harold Mozingo
Gail Murphy
M'Layne Murphy
Alice Naylor
Congregation of New
  Hope Moravian Church,
  Newton
Corinne and Russell Newell
Michelle Newton
Nancy Nicholls
Rosemary Niewold
Marilyn Norford
Northminster
  Presbyterian Church
Zona Norwood
Daintree O'Brien
Patti O'Donoghue
Debbie Paisley
Mary and George Parkerson
Marlene Payne
Camille Perotti
John A. Peterson
Weyland Plaster

Sybill Presley
Max Preston
Jane Pruden
Carol Quinn
Michele Raphoon
Allen Reep
Dianna Reid
Mary Reisch
Mary John Little Resch
Wade Reynolds
Tim Rice
Phillip D. Rich
Charles Richards
Jim Rickard
Rev. and Mrs. Burton J.
  Rights
Chris Robbins
Jane Robinson
Dawn Rogers
Leslie Rountree
Kelly Rowe
Will Rowland
Jeanne L. Rudd
Judy Rupard
Nancy St. Charles
Jim Sanders
Jim Scancerelli
Judy Scharms
Barbara Scherzer
Patsy Schneider
Carol Shaddelee
Livonia Shakelford
Janice Shearin
Cantor Shepherd
Mark Shore
Hal Silver
Naomi Simmons
Kelly Simpson
Lillian H. Simpson
Gary Smith
Jennifer Smith
Lisa Smith
Lisa Garrett Smith
Lisa Wilkins Smith
Scott Smith
Carolyn Spears
Bill and Sarah Spencer
Karen Sphar-Hope
Von Corbett Spivey
Janet Spoon
Laurel Stanell
Scotty Steele
Judy Stevens
W. B. Stronach
Marla Tamellini
Verl Thomas
Karen Thompson
Betty Currie Tilley
Dave Tomsky
Mary Lee, Daniel,
  and Emily Tosky
Claudia and Bob Touhey
Nancy Tramble
Carolyn Tucker
Richard Tuttle
Hope Tyndall
Leerae Umfleet
Denver Vance
Leslie, Paige, and

Cade Vance
Jimmy Vestal
Martha Vick
Alleene VonCanon
Jennifer and Jeremy
  Wainwright
Jan Watson
Ann Way
Kay Weaver
L. Michelle Webster
Hermann I. Weinlick
Valerie Westmoreland
Sudie Wheeler
Dolly Whisnant
Ethan Whitener
Pat Wilke
Tammy Williams
Will Willimon
Naomi Willis
Susan Wilson
Lisa Winslow
Will and Jane Wolfgang
Ardelia Womble
Lynne and Ed Wood
Patricia Houck Woods
Carole Woodward
Frank Worthington
Roger Young
Shirley Yount
David Zimmerman

## SOURCES

Cox, James A. "Keeping Christmas in the Colonies," Colonial Williamsburg: The Journal of the Colonial Williamsburg Foundations, Winter 1990-91.

Colins, Beulah "Christmas in Colonial America Marked by Round of Festivites," News of Orange County, Hillsboro, North Carolina, Dec. 21, 1967.

Jenkins, Emyl Southern Christmas, Crown Publishers, New York, 1992.

Kane, Thomas Harnett The Southern Christmas Book: The Full Story From Earliest Times, D. McKay Company, New York, 1958.

Powell, William S. North Carolina Through Four Centuries, University of North Carolina Press, Chapel Hill, 1989.

# A North Carolina Christmas Taste Test

January 6, also celebrated by liturgical churches as Epiphany (the arrival in Bethlehem of the Magi), seemed an appropriate day to hold a taste-test party for a Christmas book. Approximately 140 people were looking forward to sampling 75 delicious recipes, as well as some of the songs, poems, and stories to be included in this book. Unfortunately, Mother Nature had other plans and blanketed the city of Hickory with a deep winter snow, making travel to the Christ Lutheran Church Hall impossible (except for a handful of hardy folks who walked there), and thus canceling this exciting event. Since the dishes were already prepared, they were shared with family and friends, and comments were called in to chairpeople Robert and Patricia Kraay. I would like to offer a special thank you to the following North Carolina cooks, and their friends and families, who made this unusual taste test such a successful event after all.

*Robin Baker, Joel and Marge Barger, Lena Bengtson, Carol Bergholz, Sonja Branch, Elizabeth and Tim Bruton, Janice Buchanan, Dottie Cedar, David and Joy Crosby, Ruth Deave, Jim and Jeri Edwards, Karen Elmore, Helga and Joe Fasciano, Mary Alix Geisler, Dennis Gerami, Susan Guest, Robb Gwaltney, Charlotte Kraay, Robert and Patricia Kraay, Elsie Kussman, Audrey Lail, Ruth and Burt Long, Jim and Alice Lucas, Helen Lucks, Rowena Marion, BJ McNally, Boby and Harold Miller, Mary Puett, Lola and Leo Prough, Bryan Reiff, Kecia Roseman, Madge Roseman, Ruth Simmons, Letha and George Thomas, Lillian Tucker, Richard Tucker, Diane and Mike Urich, Susan Utsey, Sally Walters, Beth Workman, and Shirley Yount.*

## CHAMBERS OF COMMERCE

**Ahoskie**
P.O. Box 7
Ahoskie NC 27910
919-332-2042

**Albermarle/
Stanly County**
P.O. Box 909
Albermarle NC 28002
704-982-8116

**Alexander County**
104 W. Main Avenue
Taylorsville NC 28681
704-632-8141

**Alleghany County**
348 S. Main Street
Sparta NC 28675
910-372-5061

**Apex**
400 W. Williams Street
Apex NC 27502

**Archdale-Trinity**
P.O. Box 4634
Archdale NC 27263
910-434-2073

**Asheboro/
Randolph**
P.O. Box 2007
Asheboro NC 27204
910-626-2626

**Asheville Area**
151 Haywood Avenue
Asheville NC 28802
704-258-6102

**Bailey**
P.O. Box 34
Bailey NC 27807
919-235-4165

**Beaufort**
P.O. Box 56
Beaufort NC 28516
919-728-6733

**Beech Mountain**
403A Beech Mtn Pky
Beech Mountain NC
28604
800-468-5506

**Belmont**
P.O. Box 368
Belmont NC 28012
704-825-5307

**Black Mountain/
Swannanoa**
201 E. State Street
Black Mountain NC
28711
704-669-2300

**Blowing Rock**
P.O. Box 406
Blowing Rock NC 28605
704-295-7851

**Boone**
208 Howard Street
Boone NC 28607
704-264-2225

**Brevard**
P.O. Box 589
Brevard NC 28712
800-648-4523

**Bryson City/
Swain County**
P.O. Box 509
Bryson City NC 28713
704-488-3681

**Burke County**
P.O. Box 751
Morganton NC 28680
704-437-3021

**Burlington/
Alamance County**
P.O. Box 450
Burlington NC 27216
910-228-1338

**Burnsville/
Yancey County**
106 W. Main Street
Burnsville NC 28714
704-682-7413

**Caldwell County**
1909 Hickory Blvd.
Lenoir NC 28645
800-737-0782

**Carthage**
P.O. Box 540
Carthage NC 28388

**Cashiers**
P.O. Box 238
Cashiers NC 28717
704-743-5191

**Caswell County**
(see Yanceyville)

**Catawba County**
P.O. Box 1828
Hickory NC 28603
704-322-1335

**Chapel Hill**
P.O. Box 2897
Chapel Hill, NC
27515
919-967-7075

**Charlotte**
P.O. Box 32785
Charlotte NC 28232
704-377-9195

**Cherokee**
P.O. Box 465
Cherokee NC 28719
800-222-6157

**Cherryville**
P.O. Box 305
Cherryville NC 28021
704-435-3451

**Chimney Rock**
P.O. Box 32
Chimney Rock NC
28720
704-625-2725

**Clayton**
P.O. Box 246
Clayton NC 27520
919-553-6352

**Clemmons/
Tanglewood**
P.O. Box 1040
Clemmons NC 27012
910-766-0592, Press 5

**Cleveland County**
P.O. Box 794
Kings Mountain NC
28086
704-739-4755, and
P.O. Box 879
Shelby NC 28151
704-484-4999

**Clinton**
P.O. Box 467
Clinton NC 28329
910-592-6177

**Concord**
P.O. Box 1029
Concord NC 28026
704-782-4111

**Dallas**
131 N. Gaston Street
Dallas NC 28034
704-922-3176

**Denton**
Route 2, Box 66
Denton NC 27239
704-869-3574

**Dunn**
P.O. Box 548
Dunn NC 28335
910-892-4071

**Durham**
P.O. Box 3829
Durham NC 27702
919-682-2133

**Edenton/Chowan**
P.O. Box 245
Edenton NC 27932
919-482-3400

**Elizabeth City**
P.O. Box 426
Elizabeth City NC
27907
919-335-4365

**Elizabethtown**
P.O. Box 306
Elizabethtown NC 27909
910-862-4368

**Fayetteville**
P.O. Box 9
Fayetteville NC 28301
910-483-8133

**Flat Rock**
(See Hendersonville)

**Franklin**
180 Porter Street
Franklin NC 28043
704-524-3161

**Gastonia/
Gaston County**
P.O. Box 2168
Gastonia NC 28053
704-864-2621

**Goldsboro/
Wayne County**
P.O. Box 1107
Goldsboro NC 27533
919-734-2241

**Granville County**
P.O. Box 820
Oxford NC 27565
919-693-6125

**Greensboro**
P.O. Box 3246
Greensboro NC 27402
910-275-8675

**Greenville/Pitt**
302 S. Greene Street
Greenville NC 27834
919-752-4101

**Havelock**
(See New Bern)

**Hayesville/
Clay County**
P.O. Box 88
Hayesville NC 28904

**Haywood County**
Box 1079
Maggie Valley NC
28751
800-334-9036

**Henderson/
Vance County**
P.O. Box 1302
Henderson NC 27536
910-438-8414

**Hendersonville**
330 N. King Street
Hendersonville NC 28739
704-692-1413

**Hertford/
Perquimans County**
P. O. Box 27
Hartford NC 27944
919-426-5657

**Hickory/
Catawba County**
P.O. Box 1828
Hickory NC 28603
704-322-1335

**High Point**
P. O. Box 5025
High Point NC 27262
910-889-8151

**Highlands**
P.O. Box 404
Highlands NC 28741
704-526-2112

**Hillsborough**
228 S. Churton Street
Hillsborough NC 27278
919-732-8156

**Holly Ridge**
P.O. Box 364
Holly Ridge NC 28445
910-329-1515

**Huntersville**
704-875-2312

**Jacksonville/
Onslow**
P.O. Box 765
Jacksonville NC 28541
910-347-3141

**Kannapolis**
P.O. Box 249
Kannapolis NC 28082
704-932-4164

**Kenly**
P.O. Box 88
Kenly NC 27542
919-284-3431

**Kenansville**
P.O. Box 596
Kenansville NC 28349

**Kill Devil Hills**
P.O. Box 1757
Kill Devil Hills NC 27948

**Kings Mountain**
P.O. Box 794
Kings Mountain NC 28086
704-739-4755

**Kinston/
Lenoir County**
P.O. Box 157
Kinston NC 28502
919-527-1131

**Laurinburg**
P.O. Box 1025
Laurinburg NC 28353
910-276-7420

**Lenoir/Caldwell**
1909 Hickory Blvd.
Lenoir NC 28645
704-726-0323

**Lexington**
P.O. Drawer C
Lexington NC 27293
704-246-5929

**Lincolnton/
Lincoln County**
P.O. Box 247
Lincolnton NC 28093
704-735-3096

**Louisburg/
Franklin County**
P.O. Box 62
Louisburg NC 27549
919-496-2056

**Lumberton/
Robeson County**
P.O. Box 1008
Lumberton NC 28359
910-739-4750

**Madison/
West Rockingham**
112 W. Murphy Street
Madison NC 27025
910-548-6248

**McDowell**
629 Tate Street
Marion NC 28752
704-652-4240

**Mitchell County**
Route 1, Box 796
Spruce Pine NC 28777
800-227-3912

**Mocksville/
Davies County**
P.O. Box 843
Mocksville NC 27028
704-634-3304

**Montgomery County**
P.O. Box 637
Troy NC 27371
910-572-4300

**Mooresville/
S. Iredell**
P.O. Box 628
Mooresville NC 28115
704-664-3898

**Morehead City/
Carteret County**
P.O. Box 1198
Moorehead City NC 28557
919-726-6831

**Morganton/
Burke County**
P.O. Box 751
Morganton NC 28655
704-437-3021

**Mount Airy**
P.O. Box 913
Mount Airy NC 27030
800-576-0231

**Mount Olive**
123 N. Center Street
Mt. Olive NC 28365
919-658-3113

**Murfreesboro**
P.O. Box 393
Murfreesboro NC 27855
919-398-4886

**Murphy/
Cherokee County**
115 US 64 West
Murphy NC 28906
704-837-2242

**New Bern/
Craven County**
P.O. Drawer C
New Bern NC 28563
919-637-3111

**North Wilkesboro/
Wilkes County**
P.O. Box 727
North Wilkesboro NC
28659
910-838-8662

**Old Fort**
Route 1, Box 273B
Old Fort NC 28762
704-668-4244

**Oriental**
P.O. Box 472
Oriental NC 28571
919-249-0555

**Oxford/
Granville County**
P.O. Box 820
Oxford NC 27565
919-693-6125

**Pleasure Island**
201 Lumberton Avenue
Carolina Beach NC 28428
910-458-8434

**Plymouth/
Washington County**
811 Washington Street
Plymouth NC 27962
919-793-4804

**Raeford/Hoke**
P.O. Box 1260
Raeford NC 28376
910-875-5929

**Raleigh (Wake)**
P.O. Box 2978
Raleigh NC 27602
919-664-7000

**Reidsville**
P.O. Box 1020
Reidsville NC 27323
910-349-8481

**Roanoke Rapids**
P.O. Box 519
Roanoke Rapids NC 27870
919-537-3513

**Robbinsville/
Graham County**
P.O. Box 1206
Robbinsville NC 28771
704-479-3790

**Rockingham/
Richmond County**
P.O. Box 86
Rockingham NC 28380
910-895-9058

**Rocky Mount**
P.O. Box 392
Rocky Mount NC 27802
919-442-5111

**Saint Paul's**
P.O. Box 243
Saint Pauls NC 28384
910-865-3890

**Salisbury**
P.O. Box 559
Salisbury NC 28145
704-633-4221

**Sanford**
P.O. Box 519
Sanford NC 27331
919-775-7341

**Shelby/
Cleveland County**
P.O. Box 879
Shelby NC 28151
704-487-8521

**Smithfield**
P.O. Box 467
Smithfield NC 27577
919-934-9166

**Southern Pines/
Sandhills Area**
P.O. Box 458
Southern Pines NC 28388
910-692-3926

**Southport/
Oak Island**
4841 Long Beach Rd. S.E.
Southport NC 28461
910-457-6964

**Sparta/Alleghany
County**
P.O. Box 1237
Sparta NC 28675
910-372-5473

**Spencer/Rowan**
P.O. Box 165
Spencer NC 28159
704-633-4221

**Spruce Pine/
Mitchell County**
Rte. 1 Box 796
Spruce Pine NC 28777
800-227-3912

**Statesville**
P.O. Box 1064
Statesville NC 28687
704-873-2892

**Swain County**
P.O. Box 509
Bryson City NC 28173

**Swansboro**
P.O. Box 98
Swansboro NC 28584

**Sylva/Jackson County**
116 Central Street
Sylva NC 28779
704-586-2155

**Tarboro**
P.O. Drawer F
Tarboro NC 27886
919-823-7241

**Taylorsville/
Alexander County**
104 W. Main Ave.
Taylorsville NC 28681
704-632-8141

**Thomasville**
P.O. Box 727
Thomasville NC 27360
910-475-6135

**Topsall/
Pender County**
512 N. New River Drive
Topsall NC 28445
919-328-0666

**Troy/Montgomery
County**
P.O. Box 637
Troy NC 27371
910-572-2575

**Tryon/Polk**
401 N. Trade St.
Tryon NC 28782
704-859-6236

**Union County**
P.O. Box 1789
Monroe NC 28111
704-289-4567

**Valdese**
402 Main Street
Valdese NC 28690
704-879-2129

**Wadesboro/
Anson County**
P.O. Box 305
Wadesboro NC 28170
704-694-4181

**Wake Forest**
350 S. White Street
Wake Forest NC 27587
919-556-1519

**Wayne County**
(See Goldsboro)

**Waynesville**
(See Haywood County)

**Webster**
704-586-0921

**West Jefferson/
Ashe County**
P.O. Box 31
West Jefferson NC 28694
910-246-9550

**Williamston/Martin**
P.O. Box 311
Williamston NC 27892
919-792-4131

**Wilkes**
1714 Winkler Street
Wilkesboro NC 28697
910-838-8662

**Wilmington**
One Estell Lee Place
Wilmington NC 28401
910-762-2611

**Wilson/Wilson
County**
P.O. Box 1146
Wilson NC 27894
919-237-0165

**Windsor**
P.O. Box 572
Windsor NC 27983
919-794-4277

**Winston-Salem/
Forsyth County**
P.O. Box 1408
Winston-Salem, NC 27102
910-725-2361

**Wrightsville Beach**
1706 N. Lumina Ave.
Wrightsville Beach NC
28480
910-395-2965

**Yanceyville/
Caswell County**
P.O. Box 29
Yanceyville NC 27379
910-694-6106

# OTHER ADDRESSES

**Albemarle Downtown
Development Corp.**
P.O. Box 190
Albemarle NC 28002
704-982-0131

**Burlington/
Alamance County
Convention & Visitors
Bureau**
P.O. Drawer 519
Burlington NC 27216
800-637-3804

**Charlotte Convention
& Visitors Bureau**
122 E. Stonewall Street
Charlotte NC 28202
800-231-4636

**Craven County
Convention & Visitors
Bureau**
P.O. Box 1413
New Bern NC 28563
800-437-5767

**Durham Convention
& Visitors Bureau**
101 East Morgan Street
Durham NC 27701
919-687-0288

**Elizabeth City
Downtown Inc.**
P.O. Box 748
Elizabeth City NC 27907
919-338-4104

**Fayetteville Area
Convention & Visitors
Bureau**
515 Ramsey Street
Fayetteville NC 28301
910-483-5311

**Greensboro Festival
of Lights**
P.O. Box 29212
Greensboro NC 27429
910-274-4595

**Greensboro Visitor
Information Center**
317 S. Greene Street
Greensboro NC 27401
800-344-2282

**Greensboro
Preservation Society**
P.O. Box 13136
Greensboro NC 27415
800-344-2282

**Hickory Convention
& Visitors Bureau**
P.O. Box 1828
Hickory NC 28603
704-322-1335

**High Point
Convention & Visitors
Bureau**
300 S. Main Street
P.O. Box 2273
High Point NC 27261
919-884-5255

**Historic Downtown
Statesville**
P.O. Box 205
Statesville NC 28687
704-878-3436

**Matthews Historical
Foundation**
P.O. Box 1117
Matthews NC 28106
704-845-4900

**North Carolina
Christmas Tree
Association**
P.O. Box 1937
Boone NC 28607
800-562-8789

**Pinehurst, Southern
Pines, Aberdeen Area
Convention & Visitors
Bureau**
P.O. Box 2270
Southern Pine NC 28388
800-346-5362

**Raleigh Convention
& Visitors Bureau**
P.O. Box 1879, 225
Hillsborough St., #400
Raleigh NC 27602
800-849-8499

**Tanglewood Festival
of Lights**
P.O. Box 1040
Clemmons NC 27012
910-766-0592, ext. 254

**Winston-Salem
Convention & Visitors
Bureau**
P.O. Box 1408
Winston-Salem NC 27102
800-331-7018
(Christmas Line)

# ATTRACTION ADDRESSES

**Battleship
NORTH CAROLINA**
P.O. Box 480
Wilmington NC 28402
910-251-5797

**Biltmore Estate**
The Biltmore Company
One N. Pack Square
Asheville NC 28801
800-543-2961

**Caldwell Historical
Museum**
901 SW College Avenue
Lenoir NC 28645
704-758-4004

**Carl Sandburg Home
National Historic Site**
Connemara
Flat Rock NC 28731
704-693-4178

**Chinqua-Penn
Plantation**
2138 Wentworth Street
Reidsville NC 27320
910-349-4576

**Duke University
Chapel**
Box 4752, Duke Station
Durham NC 27706
919-684-2572

**Executive Mansion**
c/o Capitol Area Visitor
Center
301 N. Blount Street
Raleigh NC 27601
919-733-3456

**Fearrington House
Country Inn**
Fearrington Village Center
Pittsboro NC 27312
800-334-5475

**Fort Defiance**
P.O. Box 686
Lenoir NC 28645
704-726-0323

**Glenn Dulcimers**
631 Big Branch Road
Sugar Grove NC 28679
704-297-2297

**Greensboro
Historical Musem**
130 Summit Avenue
Greensboro NC 27401
910-373-2043

**Grove Park Inn**
290 Macon Avenue
Asheville NC 28804
800-438-5800

**Historic Hope
Foundation, Inc.**
P.O. Box 601
132 Hope House Road
Windsor NC 27983
919-794-3140

**Iredell House**
Chowan County TDA
P.O. Box 245
Edenton NC 27932

**Island Inn**
Highway 12, P.O. Box 9
Ocracoke Island NC
27960
919-928-7821

**Mast Farm Inn**
P.O. Box 704
Valle Crucis NC 28691
704-963-6934

**Museum of the
Albemarle**
1116 US 17 South
Elizabeth City NC 27909
919-335-1453

**North Carolina
Shakespeare Festival**
P.O. Box 6066
High Point NC 27262
910-841-2273

**North Carolina
Symphony**
2 East South Street
Raleigh NC 27601-2337
919-733-2750

**North Carolina
Zoological Park**
4401 Zoo Parkway
Asheboro NC 272203
800-488-0444

**The Old
Edwards Inn**
The Highlands Inn
P.O. Box 1030
Highlands NC 28741
704-526-5036

**Old Salem, Inc.**
Old Salem Museum of Early
Southern Decorative Arts
Box F, Salem Station
Winston-Salem NC 27108
910-721-7300

**Episcopal Diocese
of Western North
Carolina**
(Ben Long Frescoes)
Box 177
Glendale Springs NC
28629
910-982-3076

**Pine Crest Inn**
Pine Crest Lane
Tryon NC 28782
704-859-9135

**Richmond Hill Inn**
87 Richmond Hill Drive
Asheville NC 28806
800-545-9238

**Rocky Mount Arts
Center**
P.O. Box 4031
Rocky Mount NC 27803

**Southern Christmas
Show**
P.O. Box 36859
Charlotte NC 28236
704-376-6594

**Theatre in the Park**
107 Pullen Road
Raleigh NC 27607
919-831-6058

**Tobacco Farm
Life Museum**
P.O. Box 88
Highway 301N
Kenly NC 27542

**Tryon Palace Historic
Sites and Gardens**
610 Pollock Street
P.O. Box 1007
New Bern NC 28563
800-767-1560

**Zebulon B. Vance
Birthplace**
911 Reems Creek Road
Weaverville NC 28787
704-645-6706

**Zoo**
(See North Carolina
Zoological Park)